SCOTLAND'S NEW WRITING THEATRE

Traverse Theatre Company

Shimmer

by Linda McLean

Cast in order of appearance

Missy	Hilary Lyon
Hen	Una McLean
Petal	Lesley Hart
Sonny	Finlay Welsh
Guy	Paul Rattray
Jim	Iain Macrae

Director	Lynne Parker
Assistant Director	Lorne Campbell
Designer	Monica Frawley
Lighting Designer	Paul Keogan
Sound Designer	Fergus O'Hare
Voice Coach	Ros Steen
Stage Manager	Lee Davis
Deputy Stage Manager	Clare Burkitt
Assistant Stage Manager	Paula Donaghue

**First performed at the Traverse Theatre
Friday 30 July 2004**

TRAVERSE THEATRE

Powerhouse of new writing DAILY TELEGRAPH

Artistic Director Philip Howard

The Traverse is Scotland's new writing theatre. Founded in 1963 by a group of maverick artists and enthusiasts, it began as an imaginative attempt to capture the spirit of adventure and experimentation of the Edinburgh Festival all year round. Throughout the decades, the Traverse has evolved and grown in artistic output and ambition. It has refined its mission by strengthening its commitment to producing new plays by Scottish and international playwrights and actively nurturing them throughout their careers. Traverse productions have been seen worldwide and tour regularly throughout the UK and overseas.

The Traverse has produced over 600 new plays in its lifetime and, through a spirit of innovation and risk-taking, has launched the careers of many of the country's best known writers. From, among others, Stanley Eveling in the 1960s, John Byrne in the 1970s, Liz Lochhead in the 1980s, to David Greig and David Harrower in the 1990s, the Traverse is unique in Scotland in its dedication to new writing. It fulfils the crucial role of providing the infrastructure, professional support and expertise to ensure the development of a dynamic theatre culture for Scotland.

The Traverse's activities encompass every aspect of playwriting and production, providing and facilitating play reading panels, script development workshops, rehearsed readings, public playwriting workshops, writers' groups, discussions and special events. The Traverse's work with young people is of supreme importance and takes the form of encouraging playwriting through its flagship education project, *Class Act*, as well as the Traverse Young Writers' Group.

Edinburgh's Traverse Theatre is a mini-festival in itself THE TIMES

From its conception in the 1960s, the Traverse has remained a pivotal venue during the Edinburgh Festival. It receives enormous critical and audience acclaim for its programming, as well as regularly winning awards. In 2001 the Traverse was awarded two Scotsman Fringe Firsts and two Herald Angels for its own productions of *Gagarin Way* and *Wiping My Mother's Arse* and a Herald Archangel for overall artistic excellence. Again in 2002 the Traverse produced two award-winning shows, *Outlying Islands* by David Greig and *Iron* by Rona Munro, which both transferred to the Royal Court Theatre, London. In 2003, *The People Next Door* by Henry Adam picked up Fringe First and Herald Angel awards and transferred immediately to the Theatre Royal, Stratford East. Re-cast and with a new director, *The People Next Door* went on tour in the Spring of 2004 to England and Germany and will go on to tour to the Balkans including dates at the Belgrade International Theatre Festival in the Autumn of 2004. Raising its international profile, the Traverse will also develop projects in Japan, China, Portugal and France in 2004/05.

For further information on the Traverse Theatre's activities and history, an online resource is available at www.virtualtraverse.co.uk. To find out about ways to support the Traverse, please contact Norman MacLeod, Development Manager on 0131 228 3223.

www.traverse.co.uk • www.virtualtraverse.co.uk

FOREWORD

Shimmer is a play with its roots firmly entrenched in the muddy, drowning landscape of Scotland, yet the tiny seed for this latest work by the playwright Linda McLean was sown on the far side of the world – in Australia, to be exact. Indeed, that lyrical title is inspired by the Antipodes.

The award-winning Glaswegian writer was visiting Sydney a couple of years ago when she became intrigued by an exhibition of Aboriginal 'shimmer' paintings, which people we might call shamens – although this is not how the indigenous inhabitants of Australia would describe them – are nominated to create. 'These works of art quite literally shimmer. They transform in front of your eyes because they are made while people recount the stories of their dead in the presence of the living, who dance joyously in celebration of these past lives,' explains McLean.

'The paintings become icons, new pieces of ancestral history. As I looked at them, I thought, 'That's it! That's what you do in life after a death'. It's all about transformation. The play couldn't have had another title, because there's so much water in it anyway, it's raining all the time and, of course, it's set in Tarbet, which means 'isthmus' – a stretch of land that you can walk over and which joins the waters. So that's a writerly way for me of thinking how to get from one place to another – just like the Vikings walking with their boats on their heads in order to reach inaccessible places.'

However, *Shimmer* is not a play heavily freighted with metaphor, despite the fact that there is water everywhere in this perfectly crafted piece, which McLean began writing after the apocalyptic floods in Scotland several years ago. She is far too gifted a playwright to let her words sink under the weight of such pretentious imagery. Nonetheless, she is a profoundly beautiful, deeply reflective writer, who has frequently transmuted the salty Scots dialect into plangent poetry in works such as *Riddance*, *Olga* and *Word for Word*.

The Traverse's artistic director Philip Howard believes that few other contemporary Scots playwrights make such exquisite use of words, 'which is not to say that Linda's plays do not tell a story – they do. Her writing always follows the personal quest for its own sake'. He likens *Shimmer* to J B Priestley's 'time' plays, in which the same story is told over and over and over again, so that time appears to whirl into a vortex.

McLean herself insists that *Shimmer* is a play that could not be staged in any medium other than the theatre. 'It's precisely because this is such a highly theatrical piece that the characters, three men and three women, are given the opportunity to press the metaphorical rewind button and are able to tell their stories three times, until finally – by some trick of magic – it works and their journey is completed.'

Her six characters are therefore most definitely not in search of an author, but they are all desperately seeking something. A steady rain falls as the play begins, then the heavens open and three women – grandmother, daughter and granddaughter – fetch up at a B&B in Tarbet, that small piece of land between Loch Lomond and Loch Long. The women are on a pilgrimage to Iona in search of a miracle – twenty-something Petal is seriously ill – when they gatecrash the lives of three men, whose ages mirror those of the trio of women. 'Very Scottish, that gatecrashing!' exclaims McLean, whose Scotswomen – and men – are never remotely sentimental characters. Indeed they are often furiously funny since McLean's spare, lilting language positively fizzes with demotic energy and wit.

The journey that these three women are making is fiercely practical, firmly rooted in reality, although Shimmer is not a naturalistic play. The story is in the hands of Petal, who is trying to find a way to leave her mother and grandmother. Shimmer is therefore, on one level, a life-enhancing play about loss and allowing loved ones to depart, while still fully engaging in the business of life and remembering that life is for living. On a deeper level, though, it is a memory play, a play about how we hold people true in our hearts and minds.

Brimming with optimism, Shimmer is also that rarity nowadays, a happy play – 'perhaps my happiest play so far,' ventures McLean, who actually wrote it in the wake of great personal sadness. 'I started to write Shimmer only after I had come to a level of acceptance of some very significant deaths in my family. So I think it came out of a time when I realised I couldn't go on feeling guilty for the days when I would sometimes feel happy again – and I had found consolation in the fact that nothing is ever lost. Eventually, you realise that everybody out there is carrying this totem pole of their loved and lost with them and you recognise that those who have gone carry on informing your everyday life.'

Castlemilk-born and educated at Strathclyde University, McLean was a teacher and worked in Israel, Yugoslavia, Sweden, Kenya and the United States before turning, with considerable success, to playwriting in the early nineties. She now has a formidable body of work to her name, ranging from her powerful 1996 drama *One Good Beating*, which one critic compared to flicking backwards through a family photo album, to *Word for Word* for the Scottish company Magnetic North to *Happy Yet?*, her zesty modern take on four Feydeau farces, staged at London's Gate Theatre in the spring of 2004. She's also written for Radio 4 and Radio Scotland and has recently completed the script for a short film.

But it was McLean's 1999 drama, *Riddance*, about the way childhood trauma continues to haunt adult lives, premiered at the Traverse by Paines Plough, which established her as an important voice in Scottish theatre. Vicky Featherstone's tension-filled production, which would go on to win Fringe First and Herald Angel awards, prompted *The Scotsman*'s critic Joyce McMillan to hail 'the quality of the writing, and the strange dream-like sharpness of Linda McLean's vision'.

A prolific writer, with a deft lightness of touch that never undermines the profoundly serious and painful issues with which she engages, McLean followed *Riddance* two years later with *Olga*, a superb adaptation into rugged Scots of Finnish writer Laura Ruohonen's play about a woman of 85 and a young hoodlum of around 18 who find each other. Directed by Lynne Parker, of the renowned Irish company Rough Magic, the play was produced again in Ireland last year. Parker is also directing the world premiere of *Shimmer* since the two women have now established a truly harmonious working relationship.

Currently juggling a variety of commissions, McLean has just delivered a new play to Paines Plough for their important year-long, nine-play *This Other England* season in 2005. She is also working on a raft of new plays, two of which are commissioned and a third that she is writing 'just for myself'. *Shimmer* also began life as a play purely for herself, she confesses. 'It's a play that had a life of its own and it's one that I needed to write.' Perhaps then that is why it is such a genuinely bold and accomplished work, courageous and ambitious in its repetitive litanies of the family stories we tell in the knowledge that we are all made up of oft-told stories.

Jackie McGlone
Feature writer
June 2004

COMPANY BIOGRAPHIES

Lorne Campbell (Assistant Director) Trained: RSAMD and Liverpool John Moores. Lorne joined the Traverse in 2002 on the Channel 4 Theatre Director's Scheme. During this time he has been Director on THE NEST and Assistant Director on DARK EARTH, OUTLYING ISLANDS, MR PLACEBO, HOMERS and THE SLAB BOYS TRILOGY. Before joining the Traverse, Lorne ran Forge Theatre Company. His directing credits include: DEATH AND THE MAIDEN; THE CHEVIOT, THE STAG AND THE BLACK BLACK OIL; THE CHAIRS; THE DUMB WAITER; COMEDY OF ERRORS; OLEANNA.

Monica Frawley (Designer) Trained: National College of Art and Design, Dublin and Central St Martin's School of Art, London. Theatre includes: HEAVENLY BODIES, THE PLAYBOY OF THE WESTERN WORLD, THE GIGLI CONCERT, THE TEMPEST, TRANSLATIONS, BY THE BOG OF CATS, JUNO AND THE PAYCOCK (The Abbey and Peacock Theatres); AT THE BLACK PIG'S DYKE, ON RAFTERY'S HILL (Druid Theatre Company); DA (Guthrie Theatre, Minneapolis); CONVERSATIONS ON A HOMECOMING (Lyric Theatre, Belfast); THE DRUNKARD (b'spoke, Dublin). Film work includes: BLACK DAY AT BLACK ROCK (written and directed by Gerry Stembridge).

Lesley Hart (Petal) Trained: RSAMD. For the Traverse: OUTLYING ISLANDS, AMONG UNBROKEN HEARTS, SHETLAND SAGA. Other theatre includes: NIGHTINGALE AND CHASE, THE TWITS, A MIDSUMMER NIGHT'S DREAM (Citizens' Theatre); THE DANNY CROW SHOW (Dundee Rep); TINY DYNAMITE (Paines Plough/Frantic Assembly/Lyric Hammersmith). Television work includes: PANORAMA – INVISIBLE KIDS (BBC). Radio includes: LYNTON BAY (Radio Scotland); ANIMAL FACTS, THE MASTER OF BALLANTRAE (BBC Radio 4); BONDAGERS (BBC Radio).

Paul Keogan (Lighting Designer) Trained: The Samuel Beckett Centre, Trinity College Dublin and Glasgow University. For the Traverse: OLGA. Other work in the UK includes: BORN BAD, IN ARABIA WE'D ALL BE KINGS (Hampstead); GHOSTS, BLIND FIDDLER (Lyric Belfast); EDEN (Arts Theatre, West End & Abbey Theatre); THE TEMPEST (No 1 tour & Plymouth Theatre Royal); TOO LATE FOR LOGIC (Kings Theatre/Edinburgh Festival); THE SILVER TASSIE (Almeida). Work in Ireland includes: HEAVENLY BODIES, WILD DUCK, THE CHERRY ORCHARD, BURIAL AT THEBES, SHE STOOPS TO CONQUER, DEFENDER OF THE FAITH (Abbey Theatre, Dublin); PERFORMANCES, GATES OF GOLD (Gate Theatre, Dublin); OLGA (Rough Magic). He also works regularly in Opera & Dance and most recently on THE MAKROPOLUS CASE, UN BALLO IN MASCHERA

(Opera Zuid); JENUFA, TOSCA, THE QUEEN OF SPADES, THE
SILVER TASSIE (Opera Ireland); RITE OF SPRING (CoisCeim);
CATALYST (RexLevitates and the Chinese National Ballet).

Hilary Lyon (Missy) Trained: RSAMD. For the Traverse: THE
INNOCENT. Other theatre includes: MACBETH, AS YOU LIKE IT
(Lyric Hammersmith/English Touring Theatre); HAMLET (Donmar
Warehouse/ETT); THE SHAPE OF THE TABLE (Royal National Theatre
Studio); BONJOUR LA BONJOUR, A JOVIAL CREW (Royal National
Theatre); THE SCARLET PIMPERNEL (Wolsey Theatre); DAISY PULLS IT
OFF (Leicester Haymarket); OPERATION ELVIS, HANSEL AND GRETEL
(Citizens' Theatre/TAG); TRUMPETS AND RASPBERRIES (Borderline);
WOR JACKIE (Newcastle Playhouse) and tours with Cumbernauld,
Edinburgh Theatre Workshop, The Scottish Theatre Company and
Perth Rep. Television includes: LOVE OR MONEY, CASUALTY,
MONARCH OF THE GLEN, JONATHAN CREEK, BREAKOUT,
BETWEEN THE LINES, DANGERFIELD (series II), CHEF (series II)
(BBC); TAGGART, DOCTOR FINLAY, THIEFTAKERS, PEAK PRACTICE
(ITV). Short film includes: TUNING IN and BUTTER (Channel 4).
Hilary is currently writing a 6-part comedy drama series for Radio 4
called BAGGAGE.

Iain Macrae (Jim) Trained: Mountview Theatre School, London.
For the Traverse: HOMERS, HERITAGE, HIGHLAND SHORTS, THE
TRESTLE AT POPE LICK CREEK, LAZYBED, PASSING PLACES. Other
theatre includes: MARY, QUEEN OF SCOTS GOT HER HEAD
CHOPPED OFF (Prime Productions); BEGIN AGAIN (KTC Theatre
Company); HOUSES OF THE SEA (Tosg Theatre); PHAEDRA'S LOVE
(Ghostown/Citizens'); AIPPLE TREE (Dràma na h-Alba); SACRED
GROUND (Watford Palace); THE SLAB BOYS (Peacock Theatre);
MEMORANDUM, AFTER MAGRITTE (Zone Theatre). Television work
includes: CROWDIE AND CREAM, KILLING OF THE RED FOX,
INTERROGATION OF A HIGHLAND LASS, DWELLY, RAN DAN,
YEAR OF THE PRINCE (BBC); THE PLAN MAN (Channel 4);
MACHAIR, AIPPLE TREE, ICE CREAM MACHINE (STV). Voice for
numerous TV cartoons. Radio includes: 'P' DIVISION, DESPERATE
JOURNEY (BBC Radio Scotland); THE LETTER, NORTHERN TRAWL
(BBC Radio 4). Film includes: THE GIFT, MAIRI MHOR (BBC); AS AN
EILEAN (C4). Short films include: BEFORE WINTER WINDS,
COLOURS (BBC).

Linda McLean (Writer) Born in Castlemilk, near Glasgow, Linda
graduated and worked as a teacher in Europe, Scandinavia, Africa
and America before turning to playwriting in the early nineties. For
the Traverse: OLGA (adapted from the original Finnish play by Laura

Ruohonen), ONE GOOD BEATING. Other theatre includes: HAPPY YET? (an adaptation of four Feydeau plays for the Gate Theatre, London); WORD FOR WORD (Magnetic North); THE LAST MISSION (Edinburgh International Festival); THE LONGER NOW (Arts Ed); RIDDANCE (Paines Plough); CORRIDORS (Benchtours); THE PRICE OF A GOOD DINNER (Derby Playhouse Studio); CLIMBING THE WALLS (Ramshorn, Glasgow). Radio includes: SPIRIT'S SUNDAY DRIVE (Woman's Hour); IN THE ABSENCE OF ANGELS, TAKE ONE EGG (Radio 4). Linda will be working with new writers in Mexico City and Teluco in September 2004 and also with Det Apne Teater, Oslo, in October. In addition, she has just submitted a new commission to Paines Plough, with the working title A HIGHER PLACE.

Una McLean (Hen) Born in Strathaven and trained at RSAMD. For the Traverse: THE SLAB BOYS TRILOGY, FAMILY, THE ARCHITECT, SKY WOMAN FALLING, BLENDING IN, INES DE CASTRO. Other theatre includes: THE KERRY MATCHMAKER (Perth); THE VAGINA MONOLOGUES (EFT / Glasgow Theatre Royal); FIVE BLUE HAIRED LADIES SITTING ON A PARK BENCH (National tour, Brian Hewitt-Jones); OKLAHOMA (Perth); BEAUTY QUEEN OF LEEANE (Tron); PERFECT DAYS (Borderline); ALBERTINE IN FIVE TIMES (Clyde Unity Theatre); LOVERS, THE STEAMIE (Royal Lyceum, Edinburgh); MRS WARREN AND A PASSIONATE WOMAN (Pitlochry); BOURGEOIS GENTILHOMME (Dundee Rep); COUPLES (Cacciatore Fabbro Prods, Edinburgh Festival); REVOLTING PEASANTS (7:84); PADDY'S MARKET (Tron); ANNIE (Perth); BEGGAR'S OPERA, FIDDLER ON THE ROOF (Scottish Opera). Una has played in pantomime for 25 consecutive years, performing in CINDERELLA, SNOW WHITE, ALADDIN and BABES IN THE WOOD (to name but a few). Television work includes her own shows DID YOU SEE UNA? (STV) and the children's series BONNY! (BBC). Scottish Television profiled Una in an hour-long ARTERY special, NUMERO UNA. Film work includes: STRICTLY SINATRA (Universal Focus); NAN (Scottish Screen); THE DEBT COLLECTOR (Film Four/Pine Film); SMALL MOMENTS (The Short Film Factory). Una was awarded a Doctorate of Letters in 1995 from Edinburgh's Queen Margaret College.

Fergus O'Hare (Sound Designer) Fergus has created sound scores for numerous productions throughout the UK, the US and Europe. Recent work includes: HENRY IV (Donmar); HAMLET (Old Vic); THE QUARE FELLOW, CANDIDA (Oxford Stage Company); SINGER (Oxford Stage Company/Tricycle); THE HOLY TERROR (ATG); DANCE OF DEATH (Sydney Festival/West End); SKELLIG (Young Vic); A TASTE FOR MANGOES (Tara Arts); NOISES OFF

(West End/Broadway); A DAY IN THE DEATH OF JOE EGG (West End/Broadway); THE SHAPE OF THINGS (Almeida/Off-Broadway); CALIGULA (Donmar); THE TEMPEST (Old Vic); THIS IS OUR YOUTH (West End); UP FOR GRABS (West End).

Lynne Parker (Director) Lynne is co-founder and Artistic Director of the Dublin-based Rough Magic Theatre Company. For the Traverse: OLGA. Productions for Rough Magic include: TOP GIRLS, DECADENCE, THE COUNTRY WIFE, NIGHTSHADE, THE WAY OF THE WORLD, THE WHISPERERS, DEAD FUNNY, MIDDEN, COPENHAGEN, SHIVER, TAKE ME AWAY. Other theatre includes: HEAVENLY BODIES, THE TROJAN WOMEN, THE DOCTOR'S DILEMMA, TARTUFFE, THE SHAPE OF METAL (The Abbey and Peacock Theatres); THE HOUSE OF BERNARDA ALBA (Charabanc); THE CLEARING (Bush Theatre); THE PLAYBOY OF THE WESTERN WORLD, THE SILVER TASSIE, OUR FATHER (Almeida Theatre); THE SHADOW OF A GUNMAN (Gate Theatre, Dublin); THE IMPORTANCE OF BEING EARNEST (West Yorkshire Playhouse); THE COMEDY OF ERRORS (RSC); THE DRUNKARD (b'spoke, Dublin).

Paul Rattray (Guy) Theatre includes: COOL WATER MURDER (Belgrade); THE ANATOMIST (Royal Lyceum, Edinburgh); HAND BAG (ATC, Lyric Hammersmith); WOLFSKIN (Hardware); PLAYING THE GAME (Edinburgh Festival); DECKY DOES A BRONCO (Grid Iron); DINNER (National Theatre). Television work includes: THE BILL (ITV); SIMPLE THINGS, WET WORK (Channel 4). Film includes: MIKE BASSETT ENGLAND MANAGER (Artists Independent Network/Film Council/Hallmark Entertainment); MORVERN CALLAR (Company Pictures); ENIGMA (Broadway Pictures); MAX (Natural Nylon/ Pathe/Film Council); FURNISHED ROOM (Loud Mouse Productions Ltd). Paul has recently finished shooting the feature film CREEP (Pathe).

Finlay Welsh (Sonny) For the Traverse: THE NEST, FAITH HEALER, SHINING SOULS, AWAY, BROTHERS OF THUNDER, EUROPE, STREET FIGHTING MAN, SOMERVILLE THE SOLDIER, THE DEAD OF NIGHT, GYNT!. Other theatre includes: GAGARIN WAY (Prime Cuts, Belfast); THE ENTERTAINER (Citizens' Theatre); TRANSLATIONS, MUCH ADO ABOUT NOTHING, THE TAMING OF THE SHREW, THE ANATOMIST (Royal Lyceum, Edinburgh); MEDEA, ELECTRA, OEDIPUS, TWELFTH NIGHT (Theatre Babel). Television work includes: TAGGART (STV); THE PRACTICALITY OF MAGNOLIA (Hopscotch Films); STILL GAME (BBC). Film includes: BREAKING THE WAVES (Argus Film Produktie); TRAINSPOTTING (Channel Four Films); BEING HUMAN (BSB).

SPONSORSHIP

Sponsorship income enables the Traverse to commission
and produce new plays and to offer audiences a diverse and
exciting programme of events throughout the year. We would like
to thank the following companies for their support:

CORPORATE SPONSORS

B B C Scotland

ANNIVERSARY ANGELS

This theatre has the support of the Pearson Playwright's Scheme sponsored by Pearson plc

With thanks to

Douglas Hall of IMPact Human Resourcing for management advice arranged through the Arts & Business skills bank. Claire Aitken of Royal Bank of Scotland for mentoring support arranged through the Arts & Business Mentoring Scheme. Purchase of the Traverse Box Office, computer network and technical and training equipment has been made possible with money from The Scottish Arts Council National Lottery Fund

Scottish
Arts Council
LOTTERY FUNDED

**The Traverse Theatre's work
would not be possible without the support of**

Scottish
Arts Council

·EDINBVRGH·
THE CITY OF EDINBURGH COUNCIL

The Traverse Theatre receives financial assistance from

The Calouste Gulbenkian Foundation, The Peggy Ramsay Foundation, The Binks Trust, The Bulldog Prinsep Theatrical Fund, The Esmée Fairbairn Foundation, The Gordon Fraser Charitable Trust, The Garfield Weston Foundation, The Paul Hamlyn Foundation, The Craignish Trust, Lindsay's Charitable Trust, The Tay Charitable Trust, The Ernest Cook Trust, The Wellcome Trust, The Sir John Fisher Foundation, The Ruben and Elisabeth Rausing Trust, The Equity Trust Fund, The Cross Trust, N Smith Charitable Settlement, Douglas Heath Eves Charitable Trust, The Bill and Margaret Nicol Charitable Trust, The Emile Littler Foundation, Mrs M Guido's Charitable Trust, Gouvernement du Québec, The Canadian High Commission, The British Council, The Daiwa Foundation, The Sasakawa Foundation, The Japan Foundation

Charity No. SC002368

Sets, props and costumes for
Shimmer

created by Traverse Workshops
(funded by the National Lottery)

Scottish
Arts Council
LOTTERY FUNDED

Production photography by Douglas Robertson
Print photography by Euan Myles

**For their continued generous support
of Traverse productions the Traverse thanks**

Habitat

Marks and Spencer, Princes Street

Camerabase

BHS

Holmes Place

**For their encouragement and inspiration,
Linda McLean would like to thank**

Nicholas Bone, Jessica Dromgoole,
Vicky Featherstone, David Greig,
David Harrower, Philip Howard, Mel Kenyon,
Katherine Mendelsohn, Lynne Parker
and John Tiffany.

TRAVERSE THEATRE – THE COMPANY

SHIMMER

Linda McLean

There are some things that happened so long ago,
places or persons we have formerly seen,
of which such dim traces remain, we hardly know
whether it was sleeping or waking they occurred;
they are like dreams within the dream of life,
a mist, a film before the eye of memory . . .

William Hazlitt, 1827

For Laura

Characters

HEN, *sixties*

MISSY, *forties*

PETAL, *twenties*

SONNY, *sixties*

JIM, *forties*

GUY, *twenties*

The play takes place at a B&B in Tarbet, which sits on a small piece of land between Loch Lomond and Loch Long.

// indicates synchronicity, not necessarily a chorus. Sometimes it indicates agreement, other times the same thought said differently. The top person named has the lead voice.

. . . means a reply might be expected but doesn't materialise.

/ means interrupt.

Steady rain.

Heavier rain.

Deluge.

Inside the B&B the rain batters on the glass summer room.

SONNY *and* GUY *pass on the stairs.*

JIM, *the owner, is out of sight.*

The women: HEN, MISSY *and* PETAL *run from a train that's been stranded by flooding and fetch up outside the B&B. They look in through the glass.* PETAL *presses her nose against it.*

MISSY. This should be easy.

HEN. It might look easy to you.

MISSY. It's easy enough.

HEN. Even for me, you mean?

MISSY. Unless you make it hard.

HEN. Who?

PETAL. One, she means; unless one makes it hard.

HEN. One what?

MISSY. One person.

HEN. One galoot?
      Does she mean me?

     PETAL *separates herself from them. She wants to be our guide. Time waits for her. Outside, the rain holds its breath.*

PETAL. I'm used to things not turning out the way I want.
      Most people are. More or less. That's right, isn't it?
      Statistically speaking. A lot of people are used to things not

turning out the way they want, a small amount are used to it rarely turning out the way they want and a similarly small amount are used to it never turning out the way they want ever. I'm one of the lot of people.

These two are about to fight. Faced with a new situation, that's what they do. And what I do is try to smooth things over.

She re-engages with them. Rain as before.

HEN. . . . galoot?
Does she mean me?

PETAL. You're taking it the wrong way.

HEN. I don't know any other way to take it.

MISSY. You don't know anything.

PETAL. I've been smoothing things over for as long as I can remember. No but really, I mean, for as long as I can remember anything, this is what I've been doing. When I went to see the careers advisor at school, she asked me what I was good at and I said, 'smoothing things over. Is that a real job?' And she said, 'Yes, but you need a degree in psychology.' So that's what I'm doing now. Although so far it's been mostly statistics.

MISSY. . . . don't know anything.

HEN. I knew it was going to rain today.

MISSY. We all knew that.
It's been raining for the best part of a week.
Doesn't take a bloody psychic to look out the window.

PETAL *explains them because she doesn't want anyone to judge them too harshly. The rain pipes down but doesn't stop because it suspects she isn't going to say what it wants to hear yet.*

PETAL. Smoothing things over is interventionist, I'm told. And intervention comes in many forms. That was gentle intervention I just tried. To be honest, 'you're taking it the wrong way' doesn't always work. But empirically, it's better than 'she didn't mean that' or 'don't get upset now'. I don't know why. It's empirical.

MISSY. . . . bloody psychic.

HEN. Are you calling me an idiot?

PETAL. She didn't call you an idiot.

HEN. . . .

MISSY. . . .

PETAL. She didn't call you an idiot.

Have faith in PETAL.

Something in the way I say 'she didn't call you an idiot', which is a bland statement of the obvious, has hit a guilt button in the two of them. Something in my voice has reminded them why we're here in the first place.

MISSY. I was talking about the door.
About getting in the door.
On the surface it looks easy enough.

HEN. On one side there's us

PETAL. and on the other side there's shelter

MISSY. and the only thing between us and the other side

PETAL. is the door.

HEN. Somebody should knock it.

MISSY. We should know what we're going to say before we knock.

PETAL. We know.

HEN. We were on the train to Iona.
There was rain.

PETAL. There was a lot of rain.

HEN. There was a flood.
It would be safe to say it was a flood.
We were on the train to Iona because Petal here will die if we can't catch a miracle and there was a flood.

PETAL. You can't tell strangers I'm dying . . .

MISSY. Don't say that.

PETAL. . . . or miracle.
  Don't say miracle.

MISSY. She won't say it.
  Don't say that, you.

HEN. We were on the train to Iona.

MISSY. And don't say that either.
  The train doesn't go to Iona.
  The train only goes as far as Oban.

HEN. I know that.
  I was trying to make it less complicated.

MISSY. But it's confusing if you give wrong information.

HEN. We are going to Iona but.
  I don't think I need to get out a bloody timetable and tell
  them every stop on the line or whether there's a buffet car
  serving hot food or not.

MISSY. We're going to Oban.
  That's all anybody needs to know.
  We were on the train to Oban.

HEN. We were on the train to Oban then, and it had to stop
  because

MISSY. the track was flooded.

HEN. Okay.

PETAL. That's true

HEN. and Petal here needed a pee.

PETAL. Do you have to say that?

MISSY. She doesn't have to say that.
  Don't say that.

HEN. Okay. Okay.

MISSY. We were on the train to Oban and it had to stop

HEN. because the track was flooded

MISSY. so we thought we'd try . . .
Another way to get there?

HEN. I wouldn't let you in if you turned up on my door and
said that.

PETAL. I do actually need a pee
and it's not as if I can hold myself in.
You know that.

HEN. Right.
Just bloody knock.

MISSY. We were on the train to Oban

HEN. and it had to stop because the track was flooded and

MISSY. we wondered if we could use the phone?

PETAL. I've got a mobile.
Why would we need his phone?

HEN. Say there's no signal.

MISSY. Switch it off.

PETAL. . . . There *is* no signal.

MISSY. Jeez.

HEN. This is good.

MISSY. This is goodness.

HEN. One less lie.

PETAL. Can we knock then?

HEN. I'll knock.
I'm feeling lucky now.

She doesn't knock because suddenly it feels like a bad idea.
It is a bad idea but she doesn't know why.

I knocked on a door just like this once. It was a Sunday. But
there was no answer, at a door where I could have expected
an answer.

MISSY. Aw, don't start.

PETAL. I don't know about that door.
I'm only interested in this door.

HEN. I can't do it.
I'm not feeling lucky now.

MISSY. Well, don't look at me.
My bad luck's legendary.

HEN. Your problem is not just bad luck.

MISSY. Bad luck hasn't helped.

HEN. You're a bad picker.
Ask me.
I know about picking.

MISSY. Yes you do.

*PETAL knocks. Knock knock knock. SONNY and GUY
have heard the knocking.*

PETAL. Some things are best forgotten.

SONNY. Like the knocking that brings bad news. When you
hear it, in fact it's only when you hear it, you know you've
been expecting it. Expecting bad news is a hazard when
you're looking for someone who's gone missing. And some
might say you expect the news to be bad to protect yourself
from hurt. But no, I don't agree. The day she brought that
news, I suspected it was going to be bad, granted, but I knew
it for sure from the minute I heard the knock.

*The women begin to worry about having knocked in the first
place. PETAL knocks again. Knock knock knock.*

Is he dead? I asked her: the woman I paid to find him. (Her
name was Grey and she wore grey; I never really knew if
that was her small joke to herself or not.) I know he's dead,
I said. I heard it in the way you approached the door. In the
way you knocked. You knocked, instead of ringing. Ringing
would have meant good news. I know he's dead.

GUY. Was he dead?
Was he dead?

SONNY. He was dead.

GUY. I only ask because you said I looked like him.

SONNY. You remind me of him, is what I said.
   You remind me of him.

GUY. My face?
   My hair?
   My build?
   My teeth?

SONNY. You don't actually look like him.

GUY. But I remind you of him.

SONNY. I don't actually remember what he looks like.

GUY. Okay.
   Okay.
   You don't remember what he looks like?

SONNY. No don't.
   Don't write me off.
   I'm not / I can see what you're thinking.
   And granted, it's odd.
   I agree.
   You remind me of someone whose face I can no longer picture.
   Someone who was a young, tall, outdoors type

GUY. and dead.

   The women have begun to feel desperate with all the waiting. They've waited such a long time for other things that this waiting now seems impossible.

SONNY. Unfortunately.
   I don't know any young, tall, outdoors type any more.
   I've seen them.
   Of course I've seen them.
   They're all over the hills, and I must have passed them on the street.
   Employed them, even.
   Not personally, but I'm sure they work for me.
   I leave that to managers.

They think it's one of my strengths: delegation.
To be honest, I can't be bothered any more.
But I haven't had a conversation with a young, tall,
outdoors type for years.
Until I bumped into you at breakfast this morning.

GUY. Because it's worrying to be told that you remind
someone of his son who's dead. That's a worrying thing.
Especially since I don't even look like him, you say.
It's / well what it feels like / this is not easy but / well it
makes me wonder
Does a person carry their death around with them like
stuck-together toes?

SONNY. He didn't have stuck-together toes that I know of.

GUY. Well no, but if it ran in your family?
I mean, if you had it, it would probably run in your family.
Unless it was spontaneous, because it's one of these things,
isn't it, stuck-together toes? It's one of these things that's
been around for ever and because it doesn't kill you or
shorten your life, it just carries on, not doing anybody any
harm but then one day somebody says, somebody in your
wider family, tenth cousin twice removed, hardly even a
relation, says I've got stuck-together toes and you say, me
too and then you look at him and see that he's like you.
Maybe he's older, and losing hair and putting on weight,
and you look at him and see yourself. And see that you've
been carrying him, what he is, you've been carrying it the
whole time and you never knew.
So when you say I remind you of your son, who's dead,
I need to know why. Exactly.

PETAL *knocks again. Knock knock knock.* JIM *approaches
the door.*

JIM. It's open.

PETAL. He says it's open.

They go in. PETAL *puts her hand in her pocket and takes
out a tin. She opens it and takes a pill.*

MISSY. We've come in out of the rain.

HEN. Would you look at that . . .

MISSY. We're soaked.

HEN. . . . the door was open all the time.

MISSY. We're nearly drowned.

PETAL. You exaggerate.

HEN. Right enough.

JIM. It's always open.

MISSY. We were on the train

PETAL. yes we were on the train.

HEN. to Oban

PETAL. we were going to Oban . . .

MISSY. That's right.
I don't exaggerate.

HEN. . . . for a wee holiday and so on.

MISSY. That's right.
And the train stopped.

HEN. You might think it's odd weather for a holiday but Missy
couldn't get time off before now and Petal's had exams and,
well, this has not been an easy year for her . . .

PETAL *removes herself and talks to* JIM *but he doesn't
seem to hear her. He could, if he listened another way.*

PETAL. See. Already it's falling apart.
It's not as if they don't remember.
They do, but suddenly all the words we agreed while we
were standing in the rain don't seem to be enough.
They were, if only they'd have faith.

JIM (*to* PETAL). No, I don't . . . .
(*To* HEN.) . . . think it's odd.

HEN. . . . and I was, well, I've always wanted to go to Oban.
I had an aunt once, who lived in Oban; in fact, she's buried
there, I think, so we thought, / given

There are times when PETAL *can't quite believe that
they've forgotten her.*

PETAL. And now I'm going to burst apart at the seams; the
fear I had that I would wet myself, would make a public
show of myself, is secondary to the burning that's starting
to grip me.
(*To* HEN *and* MISSY.) Please?

MISSY. The train was flooded.

HEN. The track was flooded.

MISSY. We had to get off.

HEN. We needed a phone.

MISSY. There's no signal.

PETAL. I need to go.

HEN. It was probably the tea

MISSY. tea makes / her

HEN. she / needs to go

MISSY. go you know?

HEN. go go.

JIM. Straight along the hall and up the stairs on the left. The
key is on a nail as you go in.

PETAL *runs. They watch as she takes the key from the nail
and goes into the toilet.* MISSY *and* HEN *breathe a sigh of
relief.*

HEN. A wee holiday.

MISSY. Oban.

HEN. I don't mind the rain.

JIM. No.
It's funny.
People don't.
Not the people who come here anyway.
. . . .
Do I know you?

MISSY. No.
  I'm sorry.
  We didn't mean to barge in.

HEN. Not at all.
  That's not like us.
  Barging?
  No no.

JIM. You're sure we've never met?

MISSY. How can I say no?
  If I say no, and you remind me where, that would mean I
  didn't remember you. So.
  Have we met?

JIM. It's just that you look familiar.

MISSY. Only if you had a child in the Sick Children's Hospital
  in the last fifteen years.
  You don't have a sick child?
  Do you?

*JIM looks out through the rain-lashed windows. He sees a
blurry picture of a woman and child sitting on the grass.*

JIM. She looks like my wife. That face. That hair. That build.
  That anxious mouth. This woman, out of nowhere. Looking
  like a drowned rat. She's wandered up to my door, my door
  that I now keep open, after years of double bolts and triple
  locks, my open door, she wanders up to it and knocks. And
  stands there, drowned. Drowned, she says. An exaggeration,
  they say, but no. She looks drowned to me. Drowned and
  dripping on my flagstone floor.

PETAL knows how to listen.

PETAL. He doesn't say that out loud.

And somehow MISSY *hears something of his words.*

MISSY. Your lovely floor.

HEN. We're dripping all over it.

*JIM has been waiting for a time when his life might change.
He is beginning to think it may be today. But he's not sure.
He speaks to someone apart.*

JIM. There's a photograph of my wife and daughter sitting under a tree in the garden. Wearing dresses. I'm sure I saw them there. They spent a lot of time there, I think. I don't know if I took the photograph but I've seen it so many times now that I don't remember whether I ever really saw them there or if I only remember seeing them in the photograph.

MISSY. You don't have a sick child?

HEN. He doesn't have a sick child.
  Do you?

JIM. I don't.
  We haven't met.
  I was mistaken.
  You look like someone I know, is what it is.
  You remind me of someone.

HEN. The state she's in, it would need to be a bloody fish.

  MISSY *hears something of his confusion about forgetting and memory.*

MISSY. You get used to forgetting.

JIM. Yes.

MISSY. There comes a point when you've forgotten so much and dreamt so often that you don't know which is which.

  SONNY *and* GUY *become aware that the women need something.*

SONNY. They're very wet.

  PETAL *is stuck on the loo, unable to pee.*

PETAL. Drip.

MISSY. We're dripping all over the floor.

JIM. Don't worry about the floor.
  It's solid stone.

PETAL. Drip.

MISSY. But all this dripping.

GUY. Maybe they want a towel.

PETAL. Drip.

One minute, desperate.

Next minute, dripping.

One measly drop at a time as if it's liquid gold that can only be extracted by burning an acetylene torch on the pocket of tissue that's keeping it back so that it trickles out with a red bodyguard and cry of relief.

PETAL cries. Everything stops: the rain, the light, breathing. Something / someone presses closer. Is it now? There's a bit of a panic.

MISSY. Petal.

PETAL. Did I cry out loud?

JIM. Did you hear a cry?

MISSY. We're making a terrible puddle.

GUY. He should ask them if they want a towel.

SONNY. Take off their wet coats at least.

HEN. Did somebody mention tea?

Everything is as it was. The rain, the light, breathing. Something / someone retreats.

JIM. Tea?

HEN. The very thing.

PETAL is with them again.

MISSY. Oh there you are.

PETAL. Yes I'm here.

MISSY. Nobody mentioned tea.
(*To* JIM, *who can't hear it.*) And tea will hold us up but her life is punctuated by her tea breaks.

HEN. Give him half a chance well.

JIM. Am I the only one who heard a cry?

MISSY. It was the cry of an animal.

GUY. It was the cry of a . . . crow.

MISSY. Was it a crow?

SONNY. It's not my place.
It's actually not mine, but if it were, I'd take their coats.

MISSY. Look how we're dripping all over the beautiful floor.

HEN. Look at that.

MISSY. We should go.

HEN. We need to be going

MISSY. on our way.

HEN. We need to . . .

MISSY. be going.

> PETAL *doesn't go.*

PETAL. Your floor sparkles when it's wet.

SONNY. It's flag

JIM. flagstone.
It used to be wood.
A polished wooden floor.
So smooth and shiny that it was like standing on water.
And we're so close to the lochs that I could put my ear to
the floor and hear people calling from the boats.
Calling and laughing and and . . . and such like.

HEN. We had flagstone in our kitchen.

MISSY. When she was young.

GUY. In the olden days?

PETAL. I love flagstone.

GUY (*to someone apart*). Cunt to climb.

PETAL. He didn't say that out loud.

GUY. It splinters,

PETAL. is what he says.

HEN. The *OLDEN* days?

PETAL. I'm sure he didn't mean it that way.

HEN. I'm not so sure.

SONNY. You climb flag?

GUY. Why not?

SONNY. Ever climb it wet?

GUY. Tut.

SONNY. Of course.
  Icy?

GUY. I'm no fair-weather guy.

SONNY. Ever hear it squeal as the crampon bites in?

JIM. It's rock.

SONNY. It's more than rock.

PETAL. There are faces in those rocks.

GUY. I do that.
  Narrow my eyes and see a face.
  You can do it with almost anything.

SONNY. // Clouds.

MISSY. // Linen.

GUY. // Pizza.

HEN. Tea leaves.

SONNY. It's amazing how concentrated the mind can get when
  you're desperate

HEN. for a cuppa.

MISSY. We'll get some later.

HEN. I could be dead later.

MISSY. I doubt it.

PETAL. She says stupid things like that as if she forgets that
  it's me who'll be dead later.
  I don't say that.

That rain isn't going to get any better,
Is what I say.

JIM. Worse, I'd say.

GUY. And visibility is poor.

PETAL. It makes no odds.

MISSY. We have

GUY. to go.

SONNY *and* GUY *are in the same place as the women now.*

SONNY. I strongly advise you against it.

GUY. I know, but it's a risk I have to take.

SONNY. But you're not dressed for climbing.

MISSY. We're not climbers.

HEN. We're holiday-makers.

MISSY. Halted temporarily by a flooded train track.

HEN. We only stopped in for a

PETAL. pee

MISSY. minute

HEN. cuppa tea

MISSY. that hasn't been offered

HEN. but I'm sure is on its way.

MISSY. She's psychic like that.

HEN. I am.

PETAL. You should never have gone to see that fortune-teller woman.

HEN. She was desperate.

GUY. Fortune-tellers only tell you what you already know.

HEN. You don't know anything.

PETAL. She didn't say that.

MISSY. That fortune-teller told me to follow my instinct. She told me that I had moved so far away from trusting my own instinct that I was as good as living somebody else's life.

There's a short lull in the rain. Something / someone listens.

HEN. Whose life?

MISSY. Not yours.

SONNY. But how do you know if you're living the right life? You only get the one.

PETAL. Is that really true?

GUY. Surely you get the chance to do things differently?

SONNY. If only.

MISSY. She took one look at my hand and said, People leave you. People leave you, don't they?

ALL. . . .

MISSY. And everything I'd ever heard about fortune-tellers and their scam magic went right out the window because scam or no, when somebody can look at you for the first time and ask your question, your very own private, never before uttered-out-loud question, well, when somebody can do that, you don't really care what kind of magic they're using. And it doesn't matter if they're reading your hand or your face or your body language, all that matters is she said it out loud. People leave you.

HEN. I can't believe you just said that out loud.

The rain continues. Something / someone retreats.

MISSY. People leave you.

HEN. I'm so embarrassed.

MISSY. She thinks she owns me, so what I say reflects on her.

PETAL. But she doesn't say that out loud.
    Believe it or not.

MISSY. I don't say everything out loud.

JIM. Did somebody say they wanted tea?

HEN. See?
   Didn't I say give him half a chance?

SONNY. People leave for different reasons.

PETAL. They don't all want to go.

GUY. You're a leaver then?

PETAL. I'm a student.

SONNY. . . . builder.

MISSY. Leaver.

JIM. Is that tea for everybody?

HEN. Tea makes her go.

MISSY. He knows.

PETAL. Everybody knows now.

JIM. Well, what about coffee?

MISSY. Is it real coffee?

HEN. Real coffee?
   In a B&B?

SONNY. He's got a machine.

JIM. I can do you any kind of coffee you like.

PETAL. I don't mind.

MISSY. As long as it's not Kenco.
   I can't stand Kenco.

SONNY. // Yeah.

GUY. // Yeah.

PETAL. I really don't mind.

JIM. I've got other coffee.

MISSY. What other coffee?

JIM. I don't know.
I don't remember what it said on the tin.

MISSY. Tin?

HEN. I'm having tea.

JIM. It's a good tin.
A nice tin.
An M&S tin.

HEN. M&S?

GUY. M&S is good.

HEN. I like M&S tins.

JIM. It's good coffee inside as well.

MISSY. Is it really good coffee though?

GUY. It's good.

JIM. 'Course it's good.

MISSY. Okay.

JIM. Okay then?

MISSY. Okay.

PETAL. We staying, then?

MISSY. For a minute.

PETAL. We're staying, then.
For a minute or two.

HEN. I knew that.
I could have told you that.

JIM *almost goes to make coffees and teas. The rain is constant.* GUY *talks to someone apart.*

GUY. I'm going for a hard climb. I don't care about weather or danger. I'm on my way out but suddenly I want to stop and talk. Or steal a car and drive them where they want to go. That's not a usual thing for me. There's something about her (*Petal*). I don't know anything about her. But there's something. Something familiar.

As if someone nearby has said to him, 'You know who she reminds you of.'

You think it's that she reminds me of my mother? Thin. Blue-veined. Dark eyelids and stringy hair? Shiny when you washed it, but within hours it was lank and stringy the way mine is after a pot wash. She doesn't look like her exactly. So maybe it's the weather. I don't know. But I don't want to go now. I should go. There's little enough time as it is.

PETAL. He didn't say that.
He knew he thought it but he didn't say it out loud.

GUY *hears something of* PETAL.

GUY. You get used to not saying things out loud.

PETAL. He just looked down and sideways so I knew he was looking at me and so I had to look away. I found myself imagining the top of his thighs.
I didn't say that out loud, did I?

SONNY. Did I hear you say you were going to Oban?

HEN. Iona

MISSY. Oban

HEN. Iona

PETAL. Oban

HEN. Oban then.

GUY. You'll never get there in this rain.

SONNY. It is a lot of rain.

JIM. There's a lot of water in the rain.

GUY. And it's been raining for a long time.

And in this rain, strange things can happen. GUY *tells this to someone apart.*

At the end of my shift – I'm coming out the door, but in my head I was already in the shower – it's pissing with rain. I stink because I've been on pot wash. I don't know what I hate more, the smell of pizza or the smell of cheap detergent. A guy in a car gets out and comes towards me. I don't know him so I put my head down and move along double quick. He catches hold of me. I register that he's big before I swing for him but he stops my arm. Strong and firm but no undue pressure. He says he thinks we're related. I tell him I don't need a relation. He says something about family. I'm choked with catarrh from the kitchen. I spit on the pavement. Fucking horrible cheap detergent.

SONNY. Rain like this, you'd need a boat

GUY. 4 x 4

SONNY. helicopter

JIM. or the fish man.
  He has a van and I've never known him miss a day.

MISSY. Surely one day?

JIM. Not one single day.
  Ever.

  HEN *says this to* GUY *who doesn't know he hears it.*

HEN. There are people, aye it's true, there are people who persist. People you can depend on. They're few, and not related to me, but they exist. Jimmy Chang. He's one. Every Friday I pop into The China Sea. Jimmy Chang's wife's got a passion for chocolate gingers (the very chocolate gingers that I watch sliding by every day of the week), that just about matches my passion for the deep fried squid that Jimmy Chang's made for me every Friday night since nineteen canteen. Still keeping her sweet, I say, handing him the box. Jimmy laughs. I say the same thing every time. I tried saying something different once but it knocked him completely off kilter. He thought I was talking in code, that I needed help and kept saying, 'Evleefeeng awwight Hen, evleefeeng awwight?' Jimmy's first generation city, like I'm last. He still says 'Glesga'. We're a dying breed.

MISSY. Does he deliver on a Saturday?
  The fish man?

GUY. It's Saturday?

HEN. Sunday tomorrow.

MISSY. Genius.

PETAL. It isn't always.

SONNY. Only one day left . . .

HEN. I think she's got longer than that.

SONNY. . . . and then it's back to work.

MISSY. Oh work.

SONNY. I'm a builder by trade.
    Did I say?
    I usually do.
    I'm a man who finds solutions.
    And my office . . .
    My office is at the top of a very tall building.
    I have penthouse views over the city.
    In my other buildings I sold the top floor for the 'Aaah'
    factor, which is times ten in monetary terms. But in this
    building it just so happened, and came as a complete
    surprise to me, that I could see the zoo. I particularly like
    that zoo because of the penguins. I've a soft spot for
    penguins. (Who doesn't after *Mary Poppins*?) Certainly not
    me. Nor my son. He made me go and see it, countless
    times. 'When will it be enough?' I asked him. You know
    what he said? 'Oh you're just old, Dad.' After a minute
    I laughed. I was only thirty-five.

PETAL. You said that out loud

MISSY. which is surprising

HEN. because nice as you've looked up until now (don't forget
    he wanted to take our coats) you haven't seemed

MISSY. open.

SONNY. I don't like to think of myself as closed.
    I like to think I'm approachable.

GUY. In a business sense, you mean?
    As a boss?

SONNY. I meant as a human being.

MISSY. As a human being you never have to think in those
terms.

PETAL. As a human being

SONNY. you always have to think in those terms.

GUY. Only if you want to be approached.

HEN. He's young.

GUY. If you want to be approached you should live in a city.

HEN. He lives in a city.

SONNY. People approach him all the time.

GUY. You can't bloody move for people.

JIM. He doesn't want people that close.

MISSY. Maybe he's never been left.

GUY. I was left.

HEN. Just the once?

PETAL. Not that it's any of our business.

JIM. No but.

SONNY. It's the people who leave us we miss the most.

JIM. I miss them.

MISSY. I miss her

PETAL. even though I haven't gone yet.

SONNY. A solutions expert, you could say, is what I am.

MISSY (*to* JIM). Are you sure your fish man'll / come?

JIM. / Come hell or high water.

HEN. See?

GUY. See what?

HEN. His fish man.
    He's one of those that persist.
    Jimmy Chang's not the only one.

MISSY. Jimmy Chang's not much bloody use here, is he?

JIM. And he has a great way with fish.
They might be avoiding everybody else's nets but he always
manages to talk them onto his.
As if they're waiting for him to come get them.
Five minutes on the water and he has fish.
So you mustn't imagine he won't have any, even today.

PETAL. If this is about to turn into a fishing story, I really am
going to curl up into a ball and die, right here, right now.
Because the odds on getting to Iona were very low in the
first place. There was almost not a chance. Hen had a psychic
turn at the same time as I was reading *Cosmopolitan*. She
said,

HEN. Iona's a healing place, you know.

PETAL. Oh my god, I'm just reading about Iona, this very
minute. And I showed her, which was the worst thing I
could have done because I saw this look come over her
face; it would be fair to call it a transformation, and
suddenly there was nothing else for it but we had to rush
right over to Iona, and be healed.

MISSY. But has the fish man come in this kind of weather
before?

JIM. I don't remember this exact kind of weather before.

SONNY. 15th of January 1968.
Trees felled.
Rooftops lifted.
Waters run wild.

PETAL. You have to go a particular / route. . .

HEN. The / route runs all the way from the city to Iona

PETAL. . . . and it's been there for thousands of years.

HEN. People used to make pilgrimages along it.

MISSY. How do you know that?

HEN. My mother told me.
And I listened to my mother.

PETAL. I don't think we have time

MISSY. to waste

SONNY. spare

PETAL. for tea.

MISSY. No.

GUY. Don't go just yet.
    The fish man will come.
    Won't he?

JIM. I'd stake my life on it.

MISSY. Yours is not the life in question.
    (*To* SONNY, *who doesn't hear.*) My daughter is the one
    with the dark shadow on her bladder.

    GUY *is stunned to find that he cares so much about the*
    women. He talks to someone apart.

GUY. The fish man'll come?
    The fish man'll come?
    What the fuck do I know about the fish man?
    Why would they listen to me?
    But if I don't help, if I can't help them soon I'll have to go.
    I'll have to get out of here.

SONNY. You'd need a boat.

PETAL (*to* GUY). Do you know the fish man?

GUY. No.
    No but I know this man (*Jim*) and he's reliable.
    Isn't that right?

HEN. Don't ask me.
    I only met him today.

GUY. I thought you were psychic.

HEN. And I thought you had a mountain to climb.

PETAL. She doesn't mean it the way it sounds.

GUY. Yes she does.

MISSY. She always makes things sound worse than they really are.

HEN. Who, me?

PETAL (*to* GUY). Don't take it personally.

GUY. I don't.
It's her age.

SONNY. What did you say, son?

MISSY. You better watch yourself.

GUY. It's not an insult.
People your age were born in a depression.
It's affected you.
I've noticed.

MISSY. You mean it's not me?
I always thought it was something I did that made her bad-tempered.

GUY. Psychology has infiltrated our society in a very worrying manner.
It's almost impossible for somebody to just be a pain in the arse.

PETAL. Did you read that?

GUY. I might have.
All the same, psychology's a curse.

HEN. Great floods, plagues of locusts and the fires of hell are curses.

SONNY. And a woman scorned.

MISSY. ?

PETAL. Maybe we should just go home.

MISSY. No.

GUY *notices* PETAL*'s hands.*

GUY. And right now I see it. It's her hands. All the time it was her hands that looked familiar. She flutters them or they tremble. In the way that Mum's did just before she gave up.

I had been holding that hand for so long. I had fallen asleep
holding it. I didn't know which fingers were mine and which
were hers. When I let them go they trembled. But I had to
go to the toilet. There was nothing I could do about that.
I was seven. And while I was gone, she left. As if it was my
fault for abandoning her. I have a strong grip but I let go.

PETAL. What are you looking at?

GUY. Your hands.
They tremble.

PETAL. They've always done that.

MISSY. It doesn't mean anything.
I used to think there was some inner wire that ran through
her and every now and again something would set it off and
there she'd be, fingers trembling, knees shaking, but there
isn't a wire.

HEN *gets edgy when* MISSY *starts talking like this because
she thinks it sounds a bit weird and embarrassing.*

HEN. Okay dokay.

MISSY. No, there really isn't.
I've seen scans of her whole body.
There are no wires.

HEN. I know.

SONNY. You can never tell what's really in there.

MISSY. You can.

SONNY. Not really.

HEN. There are no wires.
Okay?

SONNY. I wasn't implying that there were.

HEN. There aren't.

SONNY. Okay.

PETAL *is starting to think that it's not going to turn out the
way she wants.*

PETAL. There's an upside to things not turning out the way
you want. When I was little and a film or a book ended
badly I'd go to bed and dream a new ending in my head. So
when the girl died or the boy had to kill his dog or the
woman only realised, too late, that she'd always loved the
man, I'd close my eyes, go back to before the bad bit, hold
the pictures in my head and re-dream it. So the girl didn't
die and the dog was saved or was never sick in the first
place and the woman told the man in time or he already
knew because someone else told him; there were any
number of ways to dream it better.

JIM. Will you be having tea, then?
And coffee?
While you wait?

MISSY. You say the fish man comes every day?

JIM. Every day.

GUY. I hate fish.

JIM. It's on the menu.
Bed and Breakfast and evening meal, fresh fish daily.
There's no point in living between two lochs if you don't
like fish.

HEN. What if you're not in?

JIM. He leaves it in the porch.
But he always knocks first. (*To* PETAL.) 'Why don't you
leave the porch door open, Jim?' he says. 'That way I can
always leave you your fish.' 'What about burglars,' I say.
'It's only the porch, what are they going to steal?' 'I don't
know. I don't know.' 'Try it then,' he says.
So I'm trying.

MISSY. Can you call him?

JIM. You want me to make the call?

MISSY. Or is that a step too far?

JIM. I don't know.
You've turned up here, out of the blue, needing shelter and

tea or coffee and now the phone and the fish man and I'm
starting to wonder where it's going to end.

SONNY (*to* HEN, *who doesn't hear*). I don't know what age
she is but she's starting to look like someone I know who
asked me for something I didn't have.

PETAL. What are you looking at?

SONNY. I don't remember.
(*To* PETAL.) When my son was born, I was mildly
disappointed. I'd wanted a girl – secretly. I'd wanted a girl
because I was concerned that I couldn't be affectionate to a
boy. I could easily picture myself cuddling a girl – well
that's normal, isn't it? – bouncing her on my knee, singing
silly nursery rhymes – all that. But it was a boy. Funniest
thing was, he was a cuddly little thing. Screamed when you
put him down. I really had no problem. All the same, a girl
would've been nice. A daughter.

MISSY. Well, what if we don't have tea?
Or coffee?
What if, instead of the tea, you phone the fish man?
And then it would only be shelter, phone and the fish man.
In fact, we could wait outside and that would make it just
the phone and the fish man?

JIM. You're making it sound like a bargain.

MISSY. You're making us sound like women who need to be
rescued.

JIM. Women do need to be rescued sometimes.

SONNY. Not in real life.

PETAL. I have to pee again.

MISSY. Are you okay?

PETAL. I have to pee.

JIM. You know where it is.
I'll get that tea.

PETAL. You don't have to.
Not just because of me.

MISSY. But will you call the fish man?

PETAL. He'll call.

> PETAL *goes quickly.* MISSY *and* HEN *talk to each other.*
> GUY *and* SONNY *talk to each other.* JIM *doesn't quite go*
> *to make tea.*

MISSY. You have to face it.

HEN. I don't.

MISSY. You do.

SONNY. You don't . . . meet many women when you're up a
mountain.

GUY. No.

HEN. No.

MISSY. She won't get to Iona today.

HEN. Is that your famous instinct kicking in?

SONNY. They're there, right enough.

GUY. But not in packs.

SONNY. And they're different when they're climbing.

GUY. Focused.

SONNY. Reliable.

MISSY. I'm not going to drag her halfway across the country
in this pissing rain when she can hardly go five minutes
without peeing herself so that you can satisfy some
ridiculous need you have for us to all think you're bloody
psychic.

SONNY. They even look different up there.

GUY. They could even be

SONNY. another species?

GUY. I know exactly

SONNY. what you mean.

HEN. It hurts you to think I might see things, doesn't it? Because that would mean that all those times I told you it was going to end in tears, it was because I could predict the future.

GUY. Off the mountain they move differently

SONNY. to a beat, you might say

GUY. a secret dance

SONNY. and only they know the steps.

GUY. Half the time you don't even know if you're in the dance

SONNY. or just meant to be

GUY. watching?

SONNY. But you definitely don't know how to do it.

MISSY (*to someone apart*). You get one chance. That's right, isn't it? You get just the one. And you might think, if you were an optimistic kind of person or a Buddhist, let's say that, if you were a Buddhist you might imagine that you're lucky. You have a body full of tricks and surprises and delights and a mind to go with it, and it'll do almost anything you ask, and give you things you didn't even know it had in it. But it's for using now, isn't that the thing about it? You use it as you go. So when you look at him and your heart flips and misses a beat, you go with that, don't you? And first time he leaves you, you cry and ache, of course you do. And you're pregnant but you get rid of it because you know you'll be crap on your own. So next time, your heart doesn't do the full flip, but you need something now, so you go again, and get pregnant again, but you have your child this time because you can't keep getting rid of them. And she's beautiful, she's the most beautiful person in your life so you never hurt her and you don't take the same chances, but then one day your heart flips again so you go with it. You always think it'll be better than the last time. Don't you?

SONNY. Up a mountain you're assured.

GUY. There's no unknown about it.

SONNY. You don't have to worry where to put your hands.

GUY. A good two / three finger space to lift from is all you
    need.

SONNY. You don't forget to breathe.

GUY. Doesn't matter how thin the air gets.

SONNY. You can look a mountain straight in the face.

GUY. It's open that way.

HEN (to SONNY, who isn't listening). I don't mince my
    words. And not because I want to be hurtful. The opposite
    in fact would be the case. But I hold out the hope that one
    of these days, she'll listen. I don't know what has to happen
    before she'll see that I've actually been looking out for her.
    That I can actually see. The real tragedy is seeing what's
    going to happen and not being able to do a damn thing
    about it. One day, I know it, one day she's going to turn to
    me and say, 'Now I understand. Thank you, Mother.' I just
    hope I live that long.

SONNY. And you can say anything to a mountain without
    feeling as though the ground drops away from you.

GUY. When the ground drops away from you up a mountain,
    you pray for a soft landing

SONNY. but you don't feel unloved.

GUY. Do you still climb?

SONNY. Not the big ones.
    More of a walker now.

GUY. Was it a fall?

    PETAL has given up trying to pee.

PETAL. The road to Iona is dotted with cairns and standing
    stones, large glittering rocks that light the way, even in
    midwinter, and there's no great distance between them.
    Given a generous amount of time, you could easily visit
    them all, touch them maybe, draw something unearthly
    from their timeless nature.

JIM. 03141 592653.

Something / someone comes closer.

MISSY. Petal, are you okay?

SONNY. Did you hear something?

PETAL. And who's to say they weren't used for celebrations as
    well as funerals. Births, marriages, that kind of thing. Who's
    to say? Maybe, on a certain day, people walked up there
    while the sun and moon were both in the sky as witnesses to
    great joy. 'I swear, in front of this hot sun and cool moon,
    that I will be with you for ever.' I can see that. I would like
    to say that.

MISSY. Was it a cry?

SONNY. I heard something.
    But no, it wasn't a cry.

MISSY. As long as it wasn't a cry.

GUY. She's been a while.

HEN. It takes her a while.

GUY. But what if she needs help

JIM. or to go again, on the journey?

GUY. Why are you going today, of all days?

PETAL. It's midsummer and on the island of Iona some
    magical quality in the light, they say, some meeting of day
    and night and sea and air at this particular time can cleanse
    or heal, whichever you need the most. And the truth is, they
    need it more than me. They've been left too often already.

SONNY. I really wouldn't advise it.

HEN. You said that before.
    And if it was any of your business, I'd tell you.
    Suffice it to say that all the signs were right.

GUY. But it's pissing down out there.

SONNY. There are floods.
    Everywhere is flooded.

There will be power cuts, for sure.
I'm amazed we haven't had one already.

HEN *tells someone apart.*

HEN. 'It's monsoon typhoon, missus,' says Jimmy. 'You goany
need a ship to go home.' 'A junk, Jimmy,' I say. 'Do you not
call it a junk?' 'Somfing like at,' he says, 'but sounds funny
like you say it. Bloody wet aw le same.' 'Bloody is an all,'
I say. 'Why you no eat hea,' he says. 'Couldn't change the
habit of a lifetime,' I say. 'How long?' he asks me. 'Must be
forty year, Jimmy,' I say. 'Must be,' he says. 'You one o le
fust peepo we meet.' 'Forty year, Jimmy, and you sound as
if you just got off the boat,' I say. 'Came on an aiaplane,
missus. Don't like boats.'

JIM. The train stopped because the line was impassable, you
said.

GUY. It's been raining for days.

HEN. These things that you're saying.
I'm not saying they're not true.
But what they are is the bad end of the good.
Can you not see that?
If you knew anything about these things, you'd know that
disasters always pre-empt a miracle.
You didn't know that?

PETAL. They didn't know that.

MISSY *speaks to someone apart.*

MISSY. In the hospital where I work there's an ultrasound
image of her bladder that has a dark patch on it. And
I remember when she was born she had a strawberry
birthmark on the back of her head that was just the same
shape. It's still there but you'd never see it, her hair's grown
over it. They're two different things but I saw them both at
that moment. I put my hand out to trace the outline of her
bladder on the screen and the radiographer turned it away.
Something between my fingers and the picture don't
connect, something that might have been important, and
I wander out into this rain.

SONNY. I've never seen a miracle.

HEN. Well, you've probably been looking in the wrong places.

PETAL *comes back.*

JIM. There you are.

PETAL. Yes, I'm here. (*To us.*) Most of the time, without being aware of it, you're catapulted from one minute into the next. Before you know anything, the tail end of one minute becomes your past and the front end of the next minute takes you smack into the future. As if your life's some dot-to-dot puzzle that somebody else drew and everybody else can see, but is invisible to you. And occasionally you get a glimpse in their faces of what lies ahead. Like now. So I'm wondering why they're looking at me like that.
(*To them.*) I'm wondering why you're looking at me like that.

GUY. You remind me of someone.

PETAL. I hope she was pretty

MISSY. and clever

HEN. and independent.

GUY. She was young.

JIM. There's no answer . . .

MISSY. No.

JIM. . . . from the fish man.
    I can't get an answer.

MISSY. Oh.

HEN. He's not coming.

GUY. You might just make it by boat.
    I'm a good sailor.
    And I'm not really afraid of the water.

PETAL. I nearly drowned once.
    I was caught under the sail.
    I couldn't go in a boat . . .

But she can't say that to JIM *without him panicking.*

JIM. You were very, very lucky you didn't drown.
Have you any idea how lucky you were?

SONNY. It would be madness.
This loch . . .

JIM. You don't know what's down there.

SONNY. . . . it's squally,
Even when there isn't a storm.

JIM. One minute, calm,
Next minute, you're fighting for your life.

PETAL. . . . and thank you for the offer . . .

GUY (*to someone apart*). If they go out in that rain, they'll
never make it. And she's trembling again. I don't know why
they have to go. Why don't they wait until the weather is
better? I know that route. I could take them. If someone
would just take her hand it might stop trembling. A firm
grasp. No one is grasping her firmly and not letting go.

SONNY. I think I could make it.
In the right vehicle.

PETAL. . . . but it's already too late

HEN. and helping is

MISSY. a mistake

SONNY. an intrusion?

JIM. Best thing would be to go home.

SONNY. Wait till it's dry.

MISSY. You don't know the best thing for her.

PETAL. I think they're right.

HEN. But we agreed.

PETAL. I know but look at them.
They're scared.

MISSY. They can't cope.

GUY. It isn't fair.

PETAL. No.
So.
We'll be on our way.

MISSY. We can see you're busy

PETAL. and we've already taken up enough of your time

MISSY. what with the fish man and the phone and the shelter and the dripping on your flagstone floor

HEN. and the tea we never got.
I knew we were never going to get that tea.

PETAL. He didn't mean anything by it.

HEN. Don't apologise for him.

PETAL (*to* JIM). She doesn't mean it.

HEN. Bloody do mean it.
I would have liked a cup of tea.
I would have liked a cup of tea very bloody much, thank you.
Because in my experience, tea is a healer.
I can't think of a bad thing in my whole life that wasn't improved by a cup of tea. Even if only marginally.
And I would be having one right now and not be quite so bloody miserable if he had just poured the water into the bloody cups.

PETAL. It doesn't matter.

PETAL, MISSY *and* HEN *are going outside.*

MISSY. The fish man's not coming, is he?
This is the one day.

GUY. I'm sorry.
I'm really sorry.

JIM. I could make the tea now.

PETAL. Really, it's fine.

MISSY. Another time, eh?

JIM. Yes. Yes.

Of course, if we had one more time to do it, we'd get it right. Wouldn't we?

PETAL. Yes come on, we'll come back another time.

JIM. And the next time, don't forget, my door's always open.

PETAL *shuts the door.*

Here they are again, running in the rain from the train towards the B&B, looking for shelter and another way to get to Iona.

HEN. Yeah, like we were ever going to get a cup of tea. I mean, how hard, is it? You boil a kettle, put tea in a pot, or if that's too hard you put a tea bag in a cup and pour boiling water over it. And hey presto. Tea. It's not bloody rocket science. You don't even have to take the tea bag out, for me. I'm not fussy. I can take it black even. It's that bloody easy, isn't it?

And here they are, standing outside the summer room. PETAL has her nose pressed against the window, as though she might see an answer.

MISSY. It might look easy to you.

HEN. It's easy enough.

MISSY. Even for me, you mean?

HEN. Unless you make it hard.

MISSY. Who?

PETAL. One, she means; unless one makes it hard.

MISSY. One what?

PETAL. One person.

HEN. One galoot?

PETAL *separates herself from them. Time waits for her. Outside, the rain holds its breath.*

PETAL. You see, I'm used to things not turning out the way I want.

MISSY (*to* HEN). Are you calling me a galoot?

She re-engages with them. Rain as before.

PETAL. I don't think she was.

MISSY. You don't know her the way I do.

HEN. You don't know anything.

MISSY. I'm going to pretend you didn't say that.
I'm going to pretend that you're not actually trying to rile me.

HEN. You were born riled.

MISSY. I wonder why?

HEN. What does she mean by that?

PETAL. Of course, the problem with intervention, they say, is that you get in the way of the natural conclusion, and you're always left wondering what would have happened if you'd just left them to it. But I've seen it too often to take that risk.
She didn't really mean it.

HEN. . . .

MISSY. . . .

PETAL. She didn't really mean it.
Something in the way I say 'she didn't really mean it' has stunned them. Because clearly she did, but something in my voice has reminded them why we're here.

MISSY. I was talking about the door.
On the surface it looks easy enough.

HEN. Somebody should knock it.

MISSY. We should know what we're going to say.

PETAL. We know.
Ever since we were told that this thing in my bladder is killing me, ever since then they've tried everything to disprove it. Funny thing was, I had almost a sense of relief when I heard it. I'd known it, you know? And there's a level of reassurance in hearing that what you know is true. Even when it's bad news. But they can't face it.

HEN. We were on the train to Iona.

MISSY. The train only goes as far as Oban.

HEN. I was trying to make it less complicated.

MISSY. But it's confusing.

HEN. We are going to Iona but.

MISSY (*to someone apart*). There's something wrong with her hard-wiring. I had this explained to me because I thought I was going mad. And I checked with other people; I spoke to her in front of witnesses just to make sure that I was actually saying what I thought I was saying (because that's another, but different hard-wiring problem). But no, sure enough I was saying what I thought. And she betrays all the signs of hearing but somewhere between her ears and her brain the words I say wander off and are replaced by words of a similar length but completely different meaning. She is pathologically incapable of duplicating an instruction.

PETAL. She can't say that out loud.

MISSY. We're going to Oban.
That's all anybody needs to know.
We were on the train to Oban.

HEN. We were on the train to Oban then, and it had to stop because the track was flooded. Okay?

MISSY. Okay.

PETAL. That's true.

HEN. And Petal here needed a pee.

PETAL. Do you have to say that?

MISSY. She doesn't have to say that. Don't say that.

HEN. But.

MISSY. We were on the train to Oban and it had to stop because the track was flooded so . . .

PETAL. I do actually need a pee.

HEN. That's right. We were on the train to Oban and it had to
stop because the track was flooded and Petal needed a pee /
okay, Petal had to go.

PETAL. Oh please.

HEN. Go go, you know.
Petal had to go and you can't, can you, when the train's
stopped.

PETAL. What happens if you go?

HEN. I don't know, do I?

PETAL. Will he mind us, using his toilet?
It doesn't feel polite.

MISSY. I thought you had to go.

PETAL. I do.

MISSY. Okay.

HEN. This is good then.
This is goodness.
One less lie.

PETAL. Can we knock then?

HEN. I'll knock.
I'm feeling lucky now.

*But she doesn't knock because something is still not right
and she still doesn't know what it is.*

I knocked on a door just like this once,

PETAL. she says, as though we have time to chat.

HEN. It was a Sunday.
But there was // no answer

MISSY. // no answer
at a door where she could have

HEN. expected an answer.
Your door.
And you were behind it.
I could hear you crying.

MISSY. She was screaming.

HEN. Jimmy Chang's wife came running over to my house.
I couldn't understand a bloody word she was saying but she
dragged me across the street and up to your door. I thought
somebody was trying to murder you. I knocked and
knocked, then shouted through the letterbox. You were lying
on the floor, half-dressed, and bawling your eyes out. And
your mother here, stark naked, hanging on to your father's
leg while he was trying to shove her off. He dragged her all
the way along the hall before he kicked her in the stomach
and pushed her away. Then he opened the door and saw me.
I thought I'd like to kill him stone-dead right where he
stood and wished I had a brick to smash his face with. Till
I looked at his face. It was pathetic. Nothing to be scared of.
He wasn't going to hurt me. I don't think he even wanted to
hurt your mother. He just couldn't get out of there fast
enough.

PETAL. I didn't know about that door.

MISSY. // We never told you.

HEN. // We never told you.

MISSY. It's not the kind of thing that crops up casually.

HEN. In fact, I think I can safely say

MISSY. the subject has never come up.

PETAL. Given the way the past leaps up at the slightest
opportunity, that must have taken superhuman effort and
concentration.

JIM, *of all of the men, is ready to listen in a different way
so he can hear something of what they say.*

JIM. // It's possible to forget a thing.

HEN. // It's possible to forget a thing

MISSY. so that you only // dream about it.

JIM. // dream about it so long

MISSY. that you come to the point where you start to forget
other things.

PETAL (*to us*). And they've started to tell me things I don't want to hear, as though they've forgotten that I won't carry them on. Things they thought might upset me before, and they don't see the non-sense of that.
I don't know about that door. I'm only interested in this door.

HEN. I can't do it.
I'm not feeling lucky now.

MISSY. Well, don't look at me.
My bad luck's legendary.

HEN. Your problem is not just bad luck.

MISSY. Bad luck hasn't helped.

HEN. You're a bad picker.
Ask me.
I know about picking.

MISSY. Yes you do.

> MISSY *knocks. Knock knock knock. Time has slipped somewhat and* GUY *hasn't met* SONNY *on the stairs and* SONNY *has gone down to speak to* JIM *about the fishing.*

PETAL. // Some things are best forgotten.

JIM. // Some things are best forgotten
because they prevent you from going forward, don't they?
Smells for example, and sounds, certain sounds.
They drag you right back.

> MISSY *knocks again. Knock knock knock.*

And you don't know they're going to have that effect until it happens.
And it hits you like a train.

SONNY. I didn't mean to bring up unpleasant memories.

JIM. No.
Of course.
You wouldn't.
And it's not fair of me to tell you, it's just that for some reason you caught me off guard.

Normally I'd never dream of discussing it.
And all you said was

SONNY. // Do you still fish?

JIM. // 'Do you still fish?'
It's probably why you came here.

SONNY. Mostly.

JIM. It's why I bought the place.
But something, I don't know, something in the way you said
it, maybe.
'Do you *still* fish?' you said.
It's the kind of question a person asks if they think you
might have stopped.
For some reason.

SONNY. I thought I was being polite.

JIM. So then, wouldn't you have said simply, 'Do you fish?'

SONNY. I think / you're

JIM. / you're right.
It was me.
It was what I heard, not what you said.

SONNY. Although now you've got me wondering why I said
'still'.

JIM. Maybe an instinct.

SONNY. I don't think so.
I don't know if I ever had that instinct but I certainly don't
have it now.

JIM. Still.

SONNY. . . . ha.

JIM. And in answer to your question, I don't fish any more.
I haven't fished since my wife and daughter drowned.

SONNY. Jesus.

JIM. I'm sorry but I couldn't leave it unsaid.
To have left it unsaid now would have meant that it would

have followed me round for ever, or at least until my next
unbroken sleep, which is probably just as distant a prospect.

SONNY (*to someone apart*). He's looking for a piece of me
that I don't have. Maybe I've never had it. I don't remember
ever feeling anything except annoyance when someone
wanted me to listen sympathetically. I've always had that
level of detachment. I don't even worry about it any more;
it's what makes me good. And it's so long since I've had to
make sympathetic gestures that I don't think I can do it
convincingly now. What's worse is I'm going to be here the
whole long weekend. If it was work, I could make it go
away, but this is my holiday time. And this unexpected rain
means I'm either going to have to spend all my time
sodden, or else hiding in my room, which is small but
comfortable, as it says in the brochure.

JIM. And now you're probably wondering how you're going to
get out of this awkward situation that I've put you in?

SONNY. No no.
No.
Not at all.

JIM. But don't worry, I won't mention it to you again.

MISSY *knocks again. Knock knock knock.*

Besides, there's someone at the door.

JIM *approaches the door with a growing sense that perhaps
he shouldn't.*

It's open.

PETAL. He says it's open.

They go in. PETAL *puts her hand in her pocket, takes out a
tin and opens it. She takes a pill.*

MISSY. We've come in out of the rain.

HEN. Would you look at that . . .

MISSY. We're soaked.

HEN. . . . . the door was open all the time.

MISSY. // We're nearly drowned.

JIM. // You're nearly drowned.

PETAL. You exaggerate.

HEN. Right enough.

JIM. It's always open.

MISSY. We were on the train

HEN. to Oban, we were going to Oban . . .

MISSY. That's right.
I don't exaggerate.

HEN. . . . for a wee holiday and so on.

MISSY. That's right, and the train stopped.

HEN. You might think it's odd weather for a sudden holiday but Missy couldn't get time off before now and Petal's had exams and, well, this has not been an easy year for her . . .

PETAL *removes herself and talks to us.*

PETAL. If I had the choice, I'd have stayed at home. But at home there's no chance of them being happy. Even less chance of them just letting me be. Every now and again, I see people making friendly gestures towards them and I start to dream about them shifting their attention away from me, just long enough for me to do what I want. Do you think that sounds odd?

JIM. No, I don't . . . think it's odd.
People come here all year round.

HEN. . . . and I was, well, I've always wanted to go to Oban. I had an aunt once, who lived in Oban; in fact, she's buried there, I think. It's a lovely story. She was a nurse and she was engaged to a doctor. A doctor in the family, now that would have been really something. And he was handsome by all accounts, although I've never seen a photograph of him. It goes like that, doesn't it? Just because he was a doctor, everybody willed him to be handsome.

PETAL. And now I'm going to burst apart at the seams; the
   fear I had that I would wet myself, would make a public
   show of myself, is secondary to the bursting that's
   threatening to explode me.
   Please?

MISSY. The train was flooded.

HEN. The track was flooded.

PETAL. Don't say flooded any more.

HEN. We had to get off.

MISSY. We needed a phone.

HEN. There's no signal.

PETAL. I need / to go.

MISSY. / She needs to go.

HEN. // Go go.

MISSY. // Go go.

JIM. Straight along the hall and up the stairs on the left.

   PETAL *is already running. They watch as she struggles
   with the key and goes into the toilet.*

   The key is on a nail . . . as you go . . . in.

   MISSY *and* HEN *breathe a sigh of relief.*

HEN. A wee holiday.

MISSY. Oban.

HEN. I don't mind the rain

MISSY. till it floods.

   They all face the rain-lashed windows. GUY *traces his
   finger down the window. Rain like this, strange things can
   happen.*

GUY. You know, in Australia, they fished a six-foot cod out of
   the water and when they cut it open it had a child inside,
   and he was still alive.

HEN. I heard that story.

MISSY. It was a man's head.

GUY. That was clearly a different cod.

SONNY. My son went to Australia.
    Have you ever been there?

GUY. I lived there for a while.

JIM. I never heard about that child.

GUY. Heads make bigger news.

JIM. // But a child.

SONNY. // But a child.

MISSY. It happens.
    And not just with cod.
    With snakes and crocodiles as well.

JIM. How did he breathe?

HEN. He must have been chewed.

MISSY. Smothered with saliva.

SONNY. Do fish have saliva?

GUY. Cod don't have teeth.
    They have suckers.

HEN. // Eeuch.

MISSY. // Eeuch.

GUY. And the boy wasn't dead. He was hardly hurt at all. And
    they were able to identify him by a birth defect: he had
    webbed feet. You know what I thought when I heard that? I
    thought the cod had saved him. That this little boy had been
    swept out of his buggy in a storm and blown into the water.
    There's a dozen things can get you in that water and one of
    them, probably a shark, or a number of sharks, were circling
    the boy. And a whole team of six-feet cod swept through
    them, at the risk of their own lives and the biggest one
    swallowed the boy. They're cold, cod, so it could feel him

cooling down, like carp, cooling down and falling into a
semi-comatose sleep. I think that big cod sought out a
fishing boat. Straight away. And offered itself up. All this in
the space of minutes. A catch like that. They'd gut it as soon
as it landed. Fishermen are curious. They know when a fish
is hiding something. And they found the boy. As soon as the
sunlight hit his body, he warmed up and opened his eyes.
The same sunlight spelled the end for the fish but before it
dried out, it heard the boy cry and saw his webbed feet.

SONNY. // Eeuch.

JIM. // Eeuch.

HEN. What's wrong with webbed feet?

GUY. That cod gave that boy a second chance.
    That boy and that cod made sense.

MISSY. Webbed feet make sense today.
    Might come in handy while we're drowning.

HEN. We're not drowning.

SONNY. You're very wet.
    Someone should do something.

PETAL. Drip.

MISSY. And we're dripping all over the floor.

JIM. Don't worry about the floor.
    It's solid stone.

PETAL. Drip.

MISSY. But all this dripping . . .

GUY. Maybe you want a towel.

SONNY. I don't think a towel is going to fix it.

GUY. It's a start.

PETAL. Just one drip.
    I'll settle for just one.
    Anything to stop the pressure building to a point where it
    will blow a hole in my back.

PETAL *cries. Everything stops: the rain, the light, breathing. Something / someone presses closer. Is this it now? Panic.*

MISSY. // Petal?

HEN. // Petal?

MISSY *knows that the cry probably means that* PETAL *did pee at last but she also knows how badly it hurts.*

JIM. // Did I cry out loud?

PETAL. // Did I cry out loud?

JIM (*to someone apart*). People used to wonder what my wife saw in me. I could see the surprise in their faces when they met her. She was a very pleasant woman with a ready smile and I was a bit of a whinger. It's hard to keep up a place like this: an old house with ancient plumbing and big rooms. Even in the summer it can get cold, and wet, as you can see. So one cold summer's day, when the central heating packed in, I went out and chopped down a tree. It was my tree, on my land; a tree that my wife and daughter used to sit under with a picnic in warm weather. Tree, woman and child, all happy as Larry, as if somehow the tree flowed into the woman and the woman flowed into the tree. So it was a tree that wasn't happy to come down and even though I hacked it to death – I made a terrible job of it – the tree kept growing under the ground and out into the loch. Endless strings of roots wound their way round legs and propeller blades. And then one day, the two of them were out on the loch when a squall got up and the boat capsized, trapping them under the sail. People said they could hear them crying all the way over to the other loch. When they fished them out, she was wrapped up in a shawl, they thought, but discovered that it was actually the roots of the tree. As though, even though she was dead, it was taking better care of her than I did. I couldn't bear to burn it after that so I brought it in and used it for the floor.

MISSY. Your beautiful floor.

PETAL *is with them again.*

HEN. Did somebody mention tea?

JIM. Tea?

HEN. The very thing.

PETAL. Nobody mentioned tea.

MISSY. You take so long.
  I get worried.

HEN. Didn't I say give him half a chance?

MISSY. We're dripping all over his beautiful floor now.

HEN. Look at that.

MISSY. We should go.

HEN. We need to be going.

MISSY. On our way.

HEN. We need to . . .

MISSY. be going.

  PETAL *doesn't go.*

PETAL. Your floor sparkles when it's wet.

JIM. It's flagstone.

HEN. We had flagstone in our kitchen.
  Every time you dropped something, it smashed.
  I never knew such an unforgiving floor.

SONNY. It's mud, you know.
  People like it as flooring.
  I find that funny.
  I'm a builder, did I say?

GUY. I could have guessed.

SONNY. What do you mean by that?

PETAL. I'm sure he didn't mean it badly.

SONNY. // I'm not so sure.

HEN. // I'm not so sure
  about that but I can assure you that the flagstone in our
  kitchen was not mud.

JIM. It's rock.
Solid impenetrable rock.

SONNY. It's more than rock.
But it started out as mud.
Lying at the bottom of a river, say, or a flood and it gets
pushed down, further and further into the earth until it gets
hot and melts and turns to rock.
People like it on floors.
I often wonder if it's because we used to have mud floors.

HEN. I never, ever, had a mud floor.
I don't know what you're implying.

GUY. // In the olden days.

PETAL. // In the olden days he meant.

HEN. ?

PETAL. The olden, olden days.
Before we were civilized.

JIM. When we lived in mud huts.

HEN. I'm not too sure about all that either.
I think it might suit some people to believe we lived in mud
huts and swung about the jungle, but I'm not one of them.

PETAL (*to us*). If she could just be happier, it would be easier
for me. I wouldn't have to feel guilty about making her
more miserable. I could start to think about leaving, how
I might leave. But instead, I have to worry about them.
It makes no odds.
// I have to go.

MISSY. // We have to go.

GUY. // I have to go.
I have a mountain to climb.

JIM. In this weather?

SONNY. I strongly advise you against it.

MISSY. // I know, but it's a risk I have to take.

GUY. // I know, but it's a risk I have to take.

SONNY. I don't want you to go.

PETAL. He didn't say that.
  He thinks he should have said it to his son but didn't.

SONNY. I don't want you to go.

PETAL. But he thought it.

MISSY. We're not climbers.

HEN. We're pilgrims.

MISSY. // ?

PETAL. // ?

HEN. Halted temporarily by a flooded train track.

HEN. // We only stopped in for a

MISSY. // We only stopped in for

PETAL. // We only stopped in for a
  pee

HEN. cuppa tea

MISSY. some directions.

SONNY. Nonetheless, something is different now and I have a
  strong suspicion that you should stay.

  SONNY *is very surprised by the strength of this urge to
  protect these women.*

  Call it an instinct – which I never thought I'd say but now
  feels like the only thing I know.

MISSY. You don't know anything about us.

PETAL. She said that out loud, which was surprising because
  it was nearly the same as asking for help.

HEN. Normally, she'd ignore something like that.

  *There's a lull in the rain. There's a hush in the landscape.
  Something / someone comes close again.*

MISSY. Normally I'd ignore something like that.

HEN. See.

MISSY. But I've been thinking, ever since I first saw you, that you remind me of someone.

SONNY (*to* MISSY, *who almost hears*). The windows on my high buildings don't open out fully; they swivel, so even if you want to stand out in a cloud or throw yourself onto some unsuspecting passer-by, you can't. My wife used to open them as wide as they'd go and turn her face up to the rain and let it kiss her. She said that about the rain kissing her face and it annoyed me. Lots of things about her annoyed me. I needed a bit of distance, I think. So I left. Funny thing was the further I got, the more I liked her. I felt the pull of her nearly as intensely as when I first knew her and couldn't maintain a distance less than five feet without being propelled towards her, in the grip of something. But I went so far for so long that she wouldn't let me back. It's too late, but I wish I'd done it differently.

PETAL. He didn't say that out loud.
He hardly knew he thought it.

SONNY. Maybe you do get the chance to do things differently.

HEN. // If only.

JIM. // If only.

MISSY. // If only.

MISSY *sees a blurry picture of a man with a boy.*

There's a photograph of my father and brother standing beside a car. Holding a football. They played football in the street. I feel sure I saw them there. They spent a lot of time there, I think. I don't know if I took the photograph but I've seen it so many times now that I don't remember whether I ever really saw them there or if I only remember seeing them in the photograph.

PETAL. She said that out loud.
Which is the first sign of hope I've had that she can see past me.

JIM. // You get used to forgetting.

MISSY. // You get used to forgetting.

GUY. // You get used to forgetting.

JIM. There comes a point
// when you've forgotten so much and dreamt so

GUY. // when you've forgotten so much and dreamt so

MISSY. // when you've forgotten so much and dreamt so

JIM. often

GUY. deeply

MISSY. clearly

JIM. that you don't know which is which

MISSY. and without corroboration an old memory becomes an old dream.

There's a chance here that things might change, if everyone can go with it.

HEN. I'm so embarrassed.

Oh well, maybe not quite yet. Rain continues. Something / someone retreats a little but not so far as before.

MISSY (*to someone apart*). She thinks she owns me, so what I say reflects on her, but I won't say that out loud. (*To* HEN.) Believe it or not, I don't say everything out loud.

JIM. // People dream for different reasons.

MISSY. // People dream for different reasons.
They don't all want to.

SONNY. You're a dreamer, then?

MISSY. I'm a nurse.

JIM. . . . B&B man

HEN. // dreamer.

SONNY. // dreamer.

HEN (*to* JIM). Did you not mention tea?

MISSY. Tea makes her go.

HEN. He knows.

PETAL. Everybody knows now.

HEN. And a wee biscuit?

MISSY. // A biscuit?

JIM. // A biscuit?

HEN. You're a B&B?
    Right?
    You must have a wee biscuit?
    Would you not like a wee biscuit, Petal?

PETAL. I'd love a biscuit.
    In fact, I've got a very strong picture of a Tunnock's teacake
    in my head right now.

HEN. You wouldn't have a Tunnock's teacake, would you?

JIM. I have got Tunnock's teacakes.
    How did you know?

HEN. I'm psychic like that.
    I bet he's got caramel wafers as well.

JIM. I have.

MISSY. Too sickly.

SONNY. Less messy.

HEN. You don't have to make a mess eating Tunnock's teacakes.

GUY. // Yeah you do.

PETAL. // Yeah you do.
    You've no option.
    Once you've cracked that top layer of chocolate, you've got
    to poke your tongue in and scoop up all the white stuff.
    It stands to reason.

GUY. See?

MISSY. I'm not really a big biscuit-eater.
    Or chocolates for that matter.

HEN. No.
You're not, are you?

MISSY. Don't take it personally.
In my profession, people are often grateful, you've nursed
their child and they want to show you how much they
appreciate you, so they bring you chocolates. I never have
the heart to say I don't like chocolates, but I appreciate the
appreciation.

JIM. I don't know.
If it were me, I'd want to give you something you liked.

MISSY. That's very nice of you.
Thank you.

JIM. It's a pleasure.

HEN. What's she thanking him for?
I hope she's not being sarcastic.

PETAL. Are we staying, then?

MISSY. For a minute.

PETAL. We're staying, then.
For a minute or two.

HEN. I knew that.
I could have told you that.

JIM *nearly goes to make the tea but is distracted by
something in the sound of the rain and the hills.*

SONNY. My son was a climber.

GUY. Was he?

SONNY. You sound a bit like him . . .

GUY. Do I?

SONNY. . . . except he shouted at the rock, whichever rock he
was climbing.
If it was giving him a hard time.
Do you shout at the rocks?

GUY. Not out loud, I don't think.

SONNY. 'Fuck you,' he'd yell.
It made me cringe.
'Open up, you bastard' – stuff like that.
Worse even.
'Give a bit, you cracking cunt' was actually the worse one
I remember.
It's why I never went climbing with him in a group.
Shouting – as if the mountain could hear.
All the way up to the top, or wherever we stopped.
'Fuck you, mountain.'
All the way.
And then as soon as we got there, he was as happy as a
sand boy.

GUY. 'You cracking cunt?'
That's strong.

MISSY. I'm surprised the mountain didn't take offence.

HEN. I'd slap his jaw good and hard if I was the mountain.

SONNY. But it was good for him.
It made him better natured.

HEN. It's all in the upbringing.
Language like that.

MISSY. Fuck off.

HEN. // I beg your pardon.

PETAL. // I beg your pardon.
I'm shocked.
I never use that kind of language to you.

SONNY. Did I hear you say you were going to Oban?

HEN. Iona.

MISSY. Oban.

HEN. // Iona.

PETAL. // Iona.

MISSY. // Iona then.

HEN. // Iona.

PETAL. // Iona.

SONNY. There's an old route from here to Iona, via Oban.

PETAL. // I know.

HEN. // I know.

SONNY. A very old route.
    A straight line.
    It goes right across the Cobbler.

GUY. Have you ever climbed the Cobbler?

SONNY. Many a time.

GUY. It's a bastard, isn't it?
    When it's icy.

PETAL. But how would someone / pilgrims, for example . . .

MISSY. Pilgrims?

PETAL. . . . in the olden days, how would they get over the
    Cobbler?

SONNY. There's always climbing involved in pilgrimages.
    Hundreds of stairs, being one that comes to mind.
    Pilgrimages, by their very nature, must be arduous.
    Besides, it's only the last bit that's hard, and they probably
    didn't go right up. You can go round.
    Near the top.
    It's not too bad.

GUY. Grassy in the summer.
    I went up there one day and saw a couple of girls sitting on
    the grass, having a picnic, reading the papers.
    They didn't even have the right shoes on.
    I gave them a look.

SONNY. Locals.

GUY. Waitresses, I think.
    They were dressed in black.
    They were wearing skirts.

JIM. Locals have a different attitude to their landscape.
    They know when it's feeling friendly.

HEN. Like the lift, in my block of flats.
　　Soon as that lift door opens, before even, you know what's
　　been going on in there.
　　You can feel it – well, smell it sometimes.
　　Sometimes I take the stairs up.

JIM. It's like the fish.

HEN. Is it?

PETAL. Are you going to tell another fishing story?

JIM. Another fishing story?
　　No.
　　It's not a story.
　　Just a thing about fish.

PETAL. Oh?

JIM. And landscape.

PETAL. Right.

JIM. It's short, ish.

PETAL. Good.

JIM. I'll bet you think that water is a fish's natural element?

PETAL. Probably, now that you mention it.

JIM. But the thing about fish is, their true element is the sky.
　　The light.
　　You probably think an ideal picture of fishing is a man in
　　waders in the river on a bright clear day?

PETAL. Yes, yes I do.
　　When I think about it, at all.

JIM. Well, you'd be wrong.
　　All that light and clear water – spells death to a fish.
　　He'll be hiding out under the shade of some leafy tree,
　　waiting for the moment when the light starts shimmering on
　　the water, creating a distraction to the fisherman's eyes, and
　　that's when the fish will shoot off up the river.

PETAL. Thank you.
　　Thank you very much.

HEN. What's she thanking him for?

MISSY. I don't know.
  I hope she's not being sarcastic.

PETAL. That's a good thing to know.

JIM. It's true.
  The fish man put me right.
  He's been fishing these lochs forever.
  There's no one knows this landscape better than the fish man.
  You can bet he won't be put off by this weather.
  I guarantee you the fish will be jumping for him.
  Even today.

MISSY. Does he fish on a Saturday?
  The fish man?
  // It's Saturday.

GUY. // It's Saturday.

SONNY. // It's Saturday.

HEN. // It's Saturday.

PETAL. // It's Saturday.

HEN. Sunday tomorrow.

GUY. Only one day left . . .

HEN. // I think she's got longer than that.

MISSY. // I think she's got longer than that.

GUY. . . . and then it's back to work.

PETAL. // Oh work.

SONNY. // Oh work.

MISSY. // Oh work.

HEN. // Oh work.

GUY. I make pizza.
  Pizza's crap but it's better than fish.
  I hate fish.
  Dead fish smells like piss.

PETAL. He said that out loud which was surprising because nice as he's looked up until now (don't forget he wanted to offer us towels), he hadn't seemed open . . .

GUY (*to* MISSY, *who doesn't hear*). For days after my mum died they kept her in a coffin in the living room. That used to be normal but now it feels weird. I made a promise to myself that this time I wasn't going to leave her. After a while, they stopped hounding me to come out. My uncle, maybe he wasn't an uncle, but that's how he seemed, he gave me in some sandwiches and stuff. There were plates of food round the clock. Now and again, when they knelt for the Our Father somebody winked at me. It was okay under there until my grandmother realised I'd been peeing her carpet for three days and she dragged me out and skelped my legs. I was only little, but I remember how wrong that was. She told me, after the funeral that I could call her Mum if I wanted.

PETAL. . . . Maybe he's shy.

HEN. Maybe he's just one of those young boys with no social skills.

MISSY. Maybe he's just young.

PETAL. Not that it's any of our business.

HEN. // No but.

MISSY. // No but.

SONNY. // No but.

JIM. // No but.

SONNY. It's the young ones we miss the most.

HEN. // I miss them.

JIM. // I miss them.

SONNY. // I miss them.

MISSY. // I miss . . . her.

GUY. // I miss . . . her.

HEN. // Even though she hasn't gone yet?

PETAL. // Even though I haven't gone yet.
And how will I ever?

MISSY. Would you know how to contact him?
Your fish man.

JIM. He comes every day.

MISSY. Will he be here soon?
Has he ever not come before?
There must be at least one day he hasn't turned up?

HEN. 2nd of January 1971.
Rangers versus Celtic.
One all. (*To someone apart.*) I went out on match nights
because there was no point in staying in and besides, the
place was empty without them. I only went across the street
to Margaret's for a blether and a wee drink. But that night
I was agitated the whole time. I've an easily agitated
disposition so I wasn't that worried at first. But it never left
me. I couldn't content myself and finally Margaret said,
'Well you're about as much fun as a wet rag, why don't you
bugger off home' – she barely got the words out before me.
As I was crossing the street, there was a funny atmosphere
as if everybody in our road was holding their breath. I got in
and put on the kettle, switched on the telly. Bad news
coming from the telly, bad news from the match – a late
goal while hundreds of men and boys were already halfway
down the stairs and they all turned back to see what
happened – see if it was their team. Is what it said that
night. Lots of men and boys trampled. And I knew it was
mine. I knew it because it was the worst thing that could
happen to me. And I'd had a very bad feeling all day. I've
never liked football but I never knew it was such a thief.

PETAL. She didn't mean that day.
She was talking about the fish man.

Something comes closer, really quite close, almost visible.
This might be the time that the wind and rain and hills and
waters and everyone we ever loved and lost has been
waiting for.

JIM. He comes every day. Except a Sunday.

(*To* MISSY.) I was fixing one of the floorboards that had
been squeaking on that particular day. Voices carry across
the water you know – laughter, squealing, that kind of thing,
squealing especially. Children squeal a lot. I don't know
why I hadn't noticed it before. They squeal when there's
nothing wrong, when they're playing, having fun. Squeal
squeal, as if they're rehearsing for the day they might need
it for real. Squeal squeal squeal. And suddenly, I wasn't
hammering the floorboard any more, I was hammering the
floor. That was some hammering. Loud. I didn't hear
anything except the hammer cracking the wood. Until I felt
a tap on the shoulder and I nearly jumped out my skin. The
fish man was standing right over me.

'I knocked,' he said. 'But you didny hear me.' We both
looked at the floor.

'A couple of trout,' he said. 'On the kitchen table.'

'Right,' I said, without even turning to look at him. 'Two's
fine.'

'Shame to waste thon wood,' he said, with an eye to the rest
of the floor. 'I'm looking to build myself a boat.'

'It's meant for a boat,' I said. 'Its heart's in the water.'

'I could lay my hands on some flagstones,' he told me.

'Ideal for just such a hallway. Off the mountains.'

And I remember how voices bounce off the mountains and
don't seep their way inside them.

'I'd lift and lay them myself,' the fish man said, by way of a
trade.

'Sounds fair enough,' I say.

I came home one day and he'd been and gone. Wood
replaced with stone. And not a sound from the waters.

He is as good as his word.

HEN. He won't be here in time for us.

The rain hums.

JIM. // How do you know that?

SONNY. // How do you know that?

HEN. I'm psychic, remember.

PETAL. // I don't think we have time

HEN. // I don't think we have time
  to wait

PETAL. for tea.

HEN. // No.

JIM. // No.

MISSY. // No.
  Stay.
  The fish man will come.
  Won't he?
  You said yourself, nobody knows this landscape better.
  If we have even half a chance of getting to Oban today, it'll
  be with him.

HEN. Has anyone even seen this fish man?

GUY. I've certainly heard of him.

SONNY. He certainly knows about fish.
  I've fished with some great men, the Tay / for example, now
  there's

HEN. . . . and we certainly haven't got time to waste on idle
  fishing chit-chat . . .

GUY. // You haven't a snowballs chance in hell of getting to
  Oban today.

PETAL. // We haven't a snowballs chance in hell of getting to
  Oban today.

MISSY. Yes we have.

HEN. . . . and just as soon as we figure out how, we'll be out
  of here.

JIM. They don't mean it the way it sounds.

HEN. Yes they do.

JIM. They sound as though they don't care when they do.

GUY. // Who me?

PETAL. // Who me?

HEN. I don't take it personally.
   It's his age.

GUY. // What did you say?

PETAL. // What did you say?

MISSY. You better watch yourself.

HEN. It's not an insult.
   People your age were born in a boom.
   It's affected you.
   I've noticed.

MISSY. You mean it's not me?
   I always thought it was something I did that made her
   indifferent.

HEN. Philosophy has penetrated our society in a very worrying
   manner.
   It's almost impossible for someone to be original.

MISSY. Did you read that?

HEN. You see?
   But I might have.
   All the same /

MISSY. // Philosophy's a curse.

JIM. // Philosophy's a curse.

SONNY. // Philosophy's a curse.

GUY. Flesh-eating zombies, plagues of Xorilian bacteria, and
   the Magna Five time warp are curses.

HEN. I heard someone say that you are what you do.

MISSY. // I think it's – you are what you eat.

PETAL. // I think it's – you are what you eat.

HEN. No.
   These were French people.
   'You are what you do,' they said.
   You know what I am?

I'm a pair of eyes, an index finger and a thumb.
And I was thinking about that one day while the chocolate
gingers slid by (I can spot a faulty chocolate ginger a mile
off so no matter how many there are in a batch and
sometimes you get a whole bad batch, but no matter how
many there are, I see them in plenty of time to pick them up
and put them in the wastage box). But what kind of a
creature is that, just two eyes, an index finger and a thumb?

JIM. Sounds like it could be a mollusc.

HEN. That would be me, then.
A mollusc.

MISSY. She said that out loud

PETAL. which is surprising

MISSY. because even though she talks a lot, she's never been
hugely

PETAL. philosophical?

HEN. I don't like to think of myself as an empty vessel.
I like to think I'm engaging.

SONNY. In a conversational sense, you mean?

JIM. As an entertainer?

HEN. I meant as a human being.

MISSY. As a human being you never have to think in those
terms.

HEN. As a human being you always have to think in those
terms
If you want to be listened to.

GUY. She's old.

PETAL. She's tired.

SONNY. If you want to be listened to, you should employ
people.

PETAL. She lives on her own.

GUY. People ignore her all the time.

JIM. Can't bloody get herself heard

MISSY. but doesn't want to be ignored.

JIM. // Maybe she's never been loved.

GUY. // Maybe she's never been loved.

SONNY. // Maybe she's never been loved.

HEN. I was loved.

JIM. Not that it's any of our business.

HEN. // No but.

SONNY. // No but.

PETAL. // No but.

MISSY. // No but.

GUY. // No but.

HEN. It's the people who love us we miss the most.

Are there voices in the rain?

SONNY (*to someone apart*). She called him 'her boy' as if he
    wasn't mine too. As if she loved him better. As if all those
    weekends out camping and climbing meant nothing. I didn't
    just take him along because it suited me; I was trying to
    show him something. He saw. He did. He never whined. He
    kept up. But I was away, that was her point. I was always
    away when the big things happened. I was away when he
    stepped off the kerb and everything was shattered. But it
    didn't matter. He was thirty-five, for chrissake. I wouldn't
    have been holding his hand. It was just the excuse she
    needed.

PETAL. We should forget about Iona and go home.

MISSY. But we've hardly tried.

HEN. We're hardly here.

SONNY. You should wait until the rain goes off, at least.
    // It can't stay like this for ever.

GUY. // It can't stay like this for ever.

JIM (*to* SONNY). 'How come you always manage to catch the
    fish,' I said to him. 'Isn't that a bit strange.'
    'That's easy,' he says. 'There's no mystery to it. It's the
    boat. It's well made. Good wood. It sings in the water. The
    fish canny resist it.'
    'It's not even a beautiful boat,' I say.
    'Beautiful enough,' he says.
    I had the crazy thought that if I ever stepped on that boat it
    would never let me go.
    Will you be having tea, then?
    And a biscuit?
    Before you go?

HEN. Only if you're making it.

JIM. I might be a while, by the time I fill the kettle and it boils
    and I put bags in cups and so on and so forth.

GUY. // Don't you have an urn?

MISSY. // Don't you have an urn?

JIM. Yes I do.
    It's on the mantelpiece.
    It has my wife's ashes in it.

GUY. // I meant an urn for boiling water. Like in

MISSY. // I meant an urn for boiling water. Like in

GUY. the Scouts

MISSY. hospital.

JIM. This is not the Scouts.
    This is a B&B.

    MISSY *knows it's not working out and is angry at* HEN.

MISSY. You don't know even what a mollusc is.

JIM. A small b&b.

HEN. Yes I do.
    It's a shell-type thing.

MISSY. It lives in the water.

SONNY. Snails don't live in water.
  Technically.

MISSY. // You don't like the water.

PETAL. // You don't like the water.

MISSY. You can barely swim.

HEN. I swim.

PETAL. Nearly.

MISSY. You nearly drowned in the bath.

HEN. That wasn't because I didn't like the water; that was
  because it was too hot.

MISSY. I saved you.

HEN. You were stupid.

MISSY. I held your head out of the water.

JIM. You should have pulled out the plug.

MISSY. If I had let her head go to pull out the plug she would
  have drowned.

JIM. The water would have run away.

MISSY. I was little.
  I didn't know it took time to drown.
  I thought I was saving her.

HEN. Well, you didn't.

GUY. // You'd hate being a mollusc.

PETAL. // You'd hate being a mollusc.

MISSY. // You'd hate being a mollusc.
  Water or no.

GUY. Molluscs are slow.

HEN. I might not like that right enough.
  I don't like waiting.

MISSY. So can we call the fish man?

JIM. Do you want me to make the call?

MISSY. I don't know.
　We've turned up here

HEN. out of the blue

MISSY. and you offer shelter and tea

HEN. with a biscuit and

MISSY. now the phone and fish man and

HEN. I'm starting to wonder

MISSY. where it's going to end

HEN. or if

PETAL. and how I'll get out of here.

HEN. I don't know what age he is but he's starting to look like
　my father

MISSY. just before he lifted me out of my chair and

HEN. slapped my legs

MISSY. kissed me.

SONNY. // What are you looking at?

JIM. // What are you looking at?

MISSY. // I don't remember.

PETAL. // I don't remember.

JIM. Well, what if I phone and you have the tea?
　And the biscuit.
　That way you'd be sheltering *while* you have the tea.
　And then it would more or less just be shelter, phone and
　the fish man.

MISSY. You're making it sound like a bargain.

SONNY. You're making us sound as if we're the ones who
　need to be rescued.

JIM. // Men do need to be rescued sometimes.

PETAL. // Men do need to be rescued sometimes.

MISSY. // Men do need to be rescued sometimes.

HEN. // Men do need to be rescued sometimes.

GUY. Not in real life.

PETAL. I have to pee again.

MISSY. Are you okay?

PETAL. I need to pee.

JIM. You know where it is.
    I'll get that tea.

HEN. No rush.

MISSY. But will you call the fish man?

PETAL. He'll

JIM. call.

   PETAL *goes quickly.*

SONNY (*to* GUY). He had stars for eyes, that's what she used
    to say. We cremated him and his mother scattered him to the
    wind where he was caught by raindrops, she said, the same
    raindrops that fell back to the ground and settled on mud
    and earth. And he would lie there, as boys do, year in, year
    out. All the time sinking lower and lower until he comes to
    a river of fire that won't burn him but will surround him and
    carry him to a place undersea where the earth is broken.
    And there he'll be spouted up into the ocean, which will
    instantly freeze him, locking him into the surrounding rock.
    And the ocean will be so moved that the rock will rise up to
    become a mountain. And in the mountain rock, the boy's
    eyes will sparkle again. So when you need him, when you
    need to feel him close, you can find him in the hills.

PETAL. He didn't say that.
    He didn't want us to know that he'd already been offered a
    rescue by a woman. A woman he'd spurned twice.

SONNY. I'm a builder,

PETAL. he said.

SONNY. Did I say?

HEN. You said.

SONNY. I used to be a dreamer.

PETAL *is stuck again. No pee. Only pain.*

PETAL. You don't stop dreaming, even if you think you're going to die, unless you're going to die immediately, although when it is immediate you don't really have time to think. That's a good thing. I can't imagine what I'd think then. I'd probably just make a noise. I find myself dreaming and . . .

MISSY *begins to feel a dread as* PETAL *dreams.*

MISSY. Petal?

JIM (*dialling*). 03141 592653. 03141 592653.

MISSY. Petal?

PETAL. . . . Occasionally I find myself wondering, well what about crispy duck and pancakes? Does this mean I won't have them any more? Or *The Sound of Music*. The film. Or Coldplay. The music. I'm getting embarrassed now because my main dream, since I was about thirteen is about my wedding. In particular my dress. I've got sketches. (And before you snigger, let me tell you I'm not as bad as my friend Lucy – she knows what her flower girl and ushers are going to be wearing.) I'll have a long veil, longer than the dress. Silk. Proper silk. Silk so fine that it's like a second skin. And the dress hanging long and heavy and straight. No puffs. And it'll be February because no one gets married in February, and early, like nine in the morning so the ice is still sparkling in the sun. But no rain. I have snowdrops, and the green of the leaves is the only colour that isn't white. Apart from my face which is translucent. And when I walk towards the groom, he reaches out because he's suddenly afraid that I'm going to disappear. But I don't. I walk beside him, fingertips touching. Both of us electrified. And the sun is in the sky and the moon is in the sky and he says, 'I will be with you forever.'

MISSY. Petal?
    Petal?

    PETAL *muffles a cry.*

GUY. She's been a while.

HEN. It takes her a while.

GUY. But what if she needs help?

JIM. Or to go again, on the journey?

GUY. Why are you going today, of all days?

SONNY. I really wouldn't advise it.

MISSY. // You said that before.

HEN. // You said that before.

GUY. But the signs are all wrong.

SONNY. There are floods.
    Everywhere is flooded.
    There will be power cuts, for sure.
    I'm amazed we haven't had one already.

JIM. The train stopped because the line was impassable.

HEN. Signs are open to interpretation.
    It all depends what you're looking for.

SONNY. What are you looking for?

HEN. I don't know but I'm sure I'll know it when I see it.

    PETAL *comes back.*

MISSY. // There you are.

GUY. // There you are.

JIM. // There you are.

SONNY. // There you are.

HEN. // There you are.

PETAL. Yes, I'm still here.
    Why are you looking at me like that?

MISSY. // You're pinched . . .

HEN. // You're pinched.

PETAL (*to us*). If I had a father like him (*Jim*), he would take
me climbing. He'd know the names of all the rocks and
where they came from and why they're all different colours
and why some look like sheets of metal and others look like
snowmen who've been turned to ice and he'd have pockets
full of pebbles and shells picked up from the beach, so that
he could say, on any day, such and such a stone came from
such and such a place and time when the temperature was
tropical or glacial . . .

MISSY. . . . and pale.

PETAL. Or a grandfather like him (*Sonny*).
Maybe a grandfather would know that kind of thing.
Maybe if I'd had a grandfather.

HEN. You all right, Petal?

PETAL. What happened to all our men?

JIM. There's no answer . . .

MISSY. // No.

PETAL. // No.

HEN. // No.

SONNY. // No.

GUY. // No.

JIM. . . . from the fish man. I can't get an answer.

MISSY. // Oh.

PETAL. // Oh.

HEN. He's not coming.

GUY. Maybe he just hasn't got a signal.

PETAL. I don't have a signal.

JIM. There you are, then.

MISSY. // I wish it were different but there's the

PETAL. // I wish it were different but there's the

HEN. // I wish it were different but there's the

HEN. weather

MISSY. light

GUY. mountain

PETAL. long road to think of.

JIM. // Of course.

SONNY. // Of course.

HEN. And it's not your problem.

PETAL. We'll get there

MISSY. one way or another.

JIM. You're mad to try.

GUY. Weather like this, you'd need a Land Rover.

HEN. Even a Land Rover wouldn't get through that flooding.

JIM. It doesn't matter I don't have a Land Rover.

GUY. // And staying is

SONNY. // And staying is

HEN. // And staying is

PETAL. // And staying is

MISSY. like waiting.

GUY. I waited once

HEN. and they never turned up.

HEN. // Never again.

GUY. // Never again.

HEN. Best thing would be to head straight back home.

MISSY. Wait till it's dry.

SONNY. Go back

MISSY. // and try again.

SONNY. // and try again.

GUY. // Look at them.

JIM. // Look at them.

SONNY. // Look at them.

PETAL. // Look at them.

HEN. // Look at them.

MISSY. // Look at them.

PETAL. They're scared.
    They can't cope.

SONNY. // It isn't fair.

GUY. // It isn't fair.

JIM. // It isn't fair.

MISSY. // It isn't fair.

HEN. // It isn't fair.

PETAL. // It isn't fair.
    Okay?

SONNY. Even though it isn't my place.

JIM. // I wish you would stay.

SONNY. // I wish you would stay.

MISSY. But we can see you're // busy

PETAL. // busy

HEN. and we've already taken up enough of your time

PETAL. what with the fish man and the phone and the shelter
    and the dripping on the floor

GUY. and the tea they never got
    and the biscuit.

PETAL. You don't have to apologise.

JIM. I could make it now.

PETAL. Really, it's fine.

PETAL, MISSY *and* HEN *are going outside.*

MISSY. Another time, eh?

JIM. Yes.

PETAL. Yes, another time.

JIM. And the next time, don't forget, my door's always open.

PETAL *closes the door.*

Here they are, once more, running in the rain from the train towards the B&B, looking for shelter, a toilet and another way to get to Iona.

HEN. Yeah, like we were ever going to get a cup of tea. I mean, how hard is it? It couldn't be any easier. It isn't hard at all . . .

And here they are, standing outside the summer room. PETAL *is looking to the hills.*

. . . unless you make it hard.

MISSY. Who's making it hard?

HEN. You have a tendency.

MISSY. I have a tendency?

HEN. Things are always hard for you.

MISSY. Things *are* hard for me.

HEN. See?

MISSY. But really, things are hard for me.
    You don't need to be a fortune-teller to see that.

HEN. Things are hard for me an all, but you won't find me hanging about with my face tripping me.

PETAL *hangs back, not really with them this time.*

MISSY. Your face has been tripping you for so long that you've got permanent misery lines running from your mouth to your chin.

HEN. They're hereditary.

MISSY. Yeah, you probably got them from your mother.

PETAL (*looking for him*). If I'd had a really old grandfather, he'd have been in the war. He'd have scars that he'd only show me on special occasions and a limp that he never talked about. He wouldn't talk about killing anyone, he'd only tell me the funny stories, like singing Christmas carols with the Germans on Christmas Day, or playing football with them on New Year's Eve, although I'm not sure which war that was. Which war was that?

HEN. You didn't want to do this in the first place, that's what's bothering you.

MISSY. No I didn't.

HEN. If it hadn't been for Petal agreeing, you wouldn't have come . . .

MISSY. No I wouldn't.

HEN. . . . because it just about kills you to think that I might / actually know something . . .

MISSY. / You don't know anything.
Not in that way.

HEN. . . . that I might actually know something that you didn't tell me.

MISSY. I told you it was going to rain today.

HEN. I already knew that.

PETAL *takes out the tin and opens it.*

PETAL (*to us*). He'd have a mole, a sticky-out mole on his forehead and when I pressed it, his tongue would pop out and it would have a silver threepenny from olden money on it. And I would try to grab it but his tongue would always disappear into his mouth first. Except every now and then he'd let me catch it . . .

She takes the pill.

HEN. You were thinking you'd go along with it so far and then things would get so bad we'd have to turn back.

MISSY. . . .

HEN. See?

MISSY. . . .

HEN. In fact, you've put a jinx on the whole expedition.

MISSY. Expedition?

As PETAL *continues with her new version of history, the rain lightens. The water on the lochs is calm. The blackness moves off the mountains.*

PETAL. . . . but I'd have to give the silver threepenny back because it had sentimental value to him, so he'd give me ten pee in exchange and we'd put on our coats and go to the paper shop where they had jars of sweets on the shelves and I'd get ten pence worth of our favourites, mints with toffee inside, and the shopkeeper would put them in a paper bag and I'd put them in my pocket and my grandfather would pat the pocket and say, 'Don't finish them now, make sure you've got some for the bus home' . . .

HEN. Don't think I'll turn back because I won't.

MISSY. No matter what?

PETAL. I need a pee.

If her landscape could put out its hand and help her, it would try now.

HEN. Knock the door then, Missy.

MISSY. I don't like to now, not now that I'm a jinx.

HEN. You knock it, Petal.

PETAL *absent-mindedly pushes the door open and knows it's the right thing to do.* SONNY *and* GUY *have met on the stair.*

SONNY. I used to climb . . .

GUY. Did you?

SONNY. . . . with my son.

GUY. Did you?

SONNY. I did, and you don't seem very well prepared.

GUY. I travel light.

SONNY. Even so.

GUY. I like to pitch myself against the elements.

SONNY. Just you against the mountain?

GUY. The mountains never give me any hassle.

SONNY. Some people think the mountains have personalities.

GUY. They're always fair to me.

PETAL *is in the hallway.*

MISSY. Petal, what are you doing?

HEN. You can't just

MISSY. walk in like that.

HEN. Come back here.
Jesus, that girl.

MISSY. Petal.

JIM *appears,* SONNY *and* GUY *are not far away.*

JIM. // It's open.

PETAL. // It's open.

JIM. It's always open.
I gave up locking it some time ago.

MISSY *and* HEN *go in.* JIM *closes the door behind them.*

MISSY. We were on the train

HEN. to Oban

MISSY. but the track was flooded so the train stopped

HEN. and Petal here had to go.

MISSY. Go go.

HEN. You know?

> PETAL *goes to the toilet before* JIM *gives her the directions. She passes* GUY *and* SONNY. *When she takes the key, the nail comes with it.*

JIM. Straight along the hall and up the . . . stairs . . . on the left. The key is . . .

MISSY. I hope you don't mind us barging in.

HEN. Petal wasn't thinking.
Normally she'd knock.

> PETAL *takes the tin out of her pocket and opens it. Inside, she puts the rusty nail and the key.*

PETAL. . . . and when we get back to the house from the sweet shop he's tired so my grandmother makes him a cup of tea, milk and three sugars, and he falls asleep in his chair. While he's sleeping I open the tin on the mantelpiece where I know he keeps the silver threepenny and in it I find a rusty nail and an old Yale key. Three moments that changed my life, he calls them.

> JIM *really looks at the two women.*

MISSY. I'm a terrible sight.

JIM. No, no.
You're not.

HEN. It's the rain.
It always makes her hair go like rats' tails.

MISSY. No it doesn't.
I've got good hair.
I'm sorry.
We'll only be a minute.
Petal will be done in a minute.

HEN. She has to pee.
She can't help it.

JIM. Is that why you came?

MISSY. Is that bad?

JIM. I just wondered.

MISSY. Oh God, look at the mess we're making on your floor.

JIM. Don't worry.
It'll dry off.

HEN. We're trying to get to Iona for midsummer.

JIM. Do you think you'll make it?

SONNY *and* GUY *see them.*

SONNY. God, they're wet.

JIM. They were on the train

MISSY. but the line was flooded so we had to get off.

GUY. Trains eh?

HEN. What?

GUY. Trains.
They've always got some reason for stopping, eh?

PETAL. And I remember that I'm not allowed in the tin and I close my hand quickly and scratch myself with the rusty nail.

PETAL *cries a muted cry. Everything inside and outside goes quiet but the rain sings louder as something / someone edges closer.*

MISSY. Did you hear something?

SONNY. No.

GUY. No.
No I didn't.
Rain.

JIM. It was music.
Someone must be playing a radio.

HEN. // Nobody heard a cry.

MISSY. // Nobody heard a cry.
Oh look at the puddle.

HEN. Have you got a mop?

JIM. I'll get one, in a minute.

SONNY. You should take their coats.

JIM. ?

GUY. Give them a towel.

MISSY. You're very kind but really we can't stay.

HEN. If you'd get me a mop I could have this floor dry in two
shakes of a lamb's tail.
A wet floor is a hazard.

PETAL. And because I cry out, my grandfather wakens up and
looks at me, pretending he's angry in one eye and twinkling
in the other. He leans forward and takes the nail from me.
That rusty old nail caught my trousers as I leapt over a
railing once and it changed my life, he said.

JIM. Don't worry about the floor.

SONNY. It's flagstone.

MISSY. Is it?

HEN. I knew that.

JIM. It's ideal for flooring.

GUY. Makes interesting climbing.

SONNY. It's not used as much as it once was.
People prefer tiles.

HEN. Amtico.

SONNY. Jumped-up linoleum, I call it.

MISSY. I've got a wooden floor.

SONNY. They're all the rage.

MISSY. The house came with a wooden floor.

HEN. She didn't lay it.

JIM. I used to have a wooden floor.

MISSY. It's very noisy.
 // Everything echoes.

JIM. // Everything echoes.
 You used to be able to hear people.
 The people out on the water.
 Calling to each other and so on.

HEN. I've got Amtico.

SONNY. No offence meant.
 I'm a builder.
 I care about materials.

HEN. I like my Amtico floor.
 It's easy to clean.
 That's very important.
 Anyway, how would I ever get flagstones up twenty-three storeys in a dodgy lift?

SONNY. Your floor probably wouldn't support them, even if you did get them up the stairs.

HEN. Well then, I think I'll probably stick with my jumped-up linoleum.

SONNY. By all means.
 It's very tough.

PETAL. Those old wooden railings had nails and splinters sticking out of them and it turns out that as he was leaving a football match he vaulted over a railing – he was a fit man for his age – and the nail caught his trousers so he had to stop, and pull his son back to wait for him . . .

SONNY. A wooden floor is nice to dance on.

MISSY. So it is, not that I dance on it much.

HEN. You can dance on Amtico.

GUY. It squeaks.

HEN. My floor doesn't squeak.
 Maybe it's your shoes.

GUY. And you've got to be careful how you clean it.
In the pizza place where I work, if you don't clean it
properly, it gets sticky.

HEN. That's poor cleaning, not poor flooring.

MISSY. When do you dance on your floor?

HEN. I dance.

MISSY. When?

HEN. You think I don't?
When do *you* dance?

MISSY. When something comes on the radio that makes me
want to.
On occasion.

HEN. Well, so do I.

MISSY. You dance to the radio on your Amtico floor in your
kitchen in your flat, twenty-three storeys up?

HEN. Yes I do.

MISSY. You surprise me.

HEN. Ha.

The landscape is very dark and very light.

SONNY. What do you dance to?

PETAL. . . . and because he pulls his son back, he isn't on the
stairs or in the tunnel when the crowd crush each other to
death. And he's there to help people who're falling because
it happens in the stairwell right next to where he's standing
and he's strong so he pulls some people up, some people
who'd never make it otherwise.

HEN. My husband and I used to dance to the Glenn Miller
band.

MISSY. You never told me that.

SONNY. 'Chatanooga Choo Choo'?

HEN. 'Pennsylvania 65000' was our favourite.
He used to kiss me on the last '0'.

MISSY. Why did you never tell me that?

HEN. I forgot.

MISSY. How could you forget?

HEN. It's a habit I got into.

GUY. I can't dance.
    Not that kind of dancing.

HEN. Anybody can do that kind of dancing.

SONNY. Jesus, son, if you can climb a mountain you can do a
    simple waltz.
    // One two three, one two three.

HEN. // One two three, one two three.

GUY. I think there's more to it than that.
    In that old-time dancing, you have to lead.
    And stuff?
    Don't you?

MISSY. I don't know.
    I never learned.

    MISSY *closes her eyes and waltzes a few steps backwards.*
    The waters begind to lap.

    But I've danced with dancers and I can follow so that I look
    as if I'm dancing.

SONNY. Leading is easy once you know the dance.

    SONNY *waltzes a few steps forwards.*

    It's just a question of deciding where you want to go a few
    moments in advance of going and letting your partner know.

MISSY. It's just a question of not thinking.

GUY. You see?
    You think that sounds easy, don't you?

PETAL. And after the match, my grandpa hurries home to find
    his wife walking the streets because she couldn't contain
    herself and when she sees them she runs faster than she
    knew she ever could and almost knocks them over because

she's had such a bad feeling all day and she was so sure
she'd never see them again that she'd already started to
shiver . . .

HEN. I saw a film of Fred Astaire, tap dancing on flagstone.
He struck sparks.

SONNY. It's brittle.

GUY. It splinters, so you have to watch when you're climbing
because the piece you're holding onto can snap right off.

MISSY. I would love to tap dance but I don't know anyone
who does that kind of thing any more.

JIM. I . . .

MISSY. What?

JIM. My mother sent me to lessons when I was a boy.
I'd forgotten.

HEN. Yeah, that forgetting thing.

JIM. I wouldn't be able to do it now.

HEN. 'Course you would.

SONNY. Your feet don't forget that kind of thing.
I haven't danced in thirty years but I know I could.

MISSY. You'll get your turn.
After this man here.

JIM. Jim, my name's Jim.

MISSY. Mine's Melissa, but she's always called me Missy.
Go on, then.

JIM. No.
I couldn't.

GUY. Do it.

JIM *sighs, then tries out a few steps.*

PETAL. . . . and after a few years my grandpa persuades my
Grandma Hen to give up her job in the chocolate factory
and go back to school, because she wasn't a stupid woman

and he was worried that if she didn't achieve something, she might get bitter. He could help with the house and if they were careful they'd have enough left over for a sit-in meal at Jimmy Chang's now and again.

GUY. Look at that.

SONNY. You're doing it.

JIM. I'm terrible.
  I don't remember anything.

MISSY. Could you show me?

JIM. I'm too embarrassed.

HEN. Away you go.

MISSY. I'll pay attention.

HEN. She's a quick learner.
  A bad picker, but a quick learner.

MISSY. Oh please.
  Don't start.

HEN. She came to work in the factory in the summer holidays one year.
  Couldn't tell a chocolate ginger from a strawberry surprise.
  I've never been so embarrassed.

MISSY. I don't like chocolate gingers.

GUY. I love them.

MISSY. They nip.

SONNY. They're an acquired taste.

MISSY. Just a few steps.
  Go on.

  JIM *stands behind* MISSY *and shows her where to put her feet.*

PETAL. So when their daughter Melissa, my mum, is training to be a nurse, her mother's studying as well and they make cups of tea for each other, and test each other and they don't let each other away with any mistakes because they know

the tougher they are, the better they'll know their subject
and my grandfather calls them his little brainboxes . . .

MISSY *learns quickly and can do a few rudimentary steps.
Everybody claps and she bows.*

MISSY (*to* SONNY). Now you.

SONNY. No siree.

MISSY. Now Mother, would you have ever said this man
looked like a coward?

HEN. Well, maybe not to his face.
He's a man of some stature.

SONNY. I used to be lighter.

HEN. We all did . . . mister . . . (*Invites him to say his name.*)

SONNY. My real name is Anthony.
But when I was a boy I smiled all the time, believe it or not.
So they called me Sonny.
It just kind of stuck.

JIM. I can see that.

SONNY. Can you?

JIM. Now that you say it.
Now that you're smiling.

SONNY. Isn't that funny?
(*To* GUY.) Can you see it?

GUY. I'm not a good judge.
I tend not to look too closely at people.

SONNY. You're being diplomatic.

HEN. I wouldn't have said he was the diplomatic type.

GUY. And you'd be right.

HEN. I'm a terrible one for straight-talking.

MISSY. That's for sure.

HEN. I don't like pretence.

GUY. I can see that.

PETAL. . . . and he brings them biscuits for their tea and they
say, 'Are you trying to fatten us up' and he says, 'That's
right, I'm trying to fatten you up so nobody else will want
you.' But of course that isn't true and one day his wife, my
Grandma Hen, whose name is really Henrietta but she'd kill
anyone who called her that because it's far too highfalutin,
one day she catches him as he comes in from work and
says, 'Guess what?' 'What?' he says because he has no way
of knowing what she's going to say. 'Guess what our
Missy's brought home from the hospital?' and he says,
'Whatever it is, I hope it's not infectious.' So she slaps him
and says, 'She's just brought home a doctor, that's all,' and
rubs her hands with glee.

HEN. Start off pretending, pretty soon you don't know the
difference between what's real and what isn't.

JIM. What's wrong with that?
Real's not all it's cracked up to be.

MISSY. I know what you mean.
There are times when /

JIM. I know exactly what you're going to say.

HEN. It just never seemed like an option to me to fool myself.

GUY. I'm not big on pretence either.

SONNY. Now isn't that funny?

GUY. How funny?

SONNY. Interesting, is what I mean.
It's interesting.
I'd never have put the two of you in a category, but look
at that.
In the category of straight-talkers, you're a pair.

HEN. Yeah, but I can dance.
At least, I used to be able to dance.

GUY. I didn't say I couldn't dance.

MISSY. Oh yes?

GUY. Of course I can dance.

HEN. Dance with me, then.

GUY. I don't do that kind of dancing.

SONNY. What kind do you do?

GUY. It's a solo kind of dancing.

HEN. Solo dancing?
    You mean you don't have a partner?

GUY. There are other people dancing.
    Of course there are.
    I wouldn't stand on a dance floor if there was no one else
    there and dance on my own. And you can have a partner if
    you want, or if you can get one, but you don't need one.
    You find a space for yourself in the middle of all the other
    dancers and do your own thing.

JIM. So you don't have to be a wallflower.

GUY. ?

JIM. The guy who stands around the dance floor, too afraid to
    ask the girl he likes to dance.

GUY. No, you don't have to be one of them.

PETAL. My grandfather isn't sure about this doctor chappie.
    He's very polite and he's got a car and lots of doctorly
    trappings, but he doesn't seem open. My grandpa likes to
    know who you are so he can decide how long he'll put up
    with you, or whether he'll help you or not because what he
    says is everybody needs help at one time or another.
    Something about this doctor chap gives him the feeling that
    one day he'll just up and off with his Missy and they'll go
    somewhere distant and he'll lose her.

MISSY. In this solo dancing . . .

GUY. Yes?

MISSY. . . . do you go alone?

GUY. You can go on your own.

JIM. Can you?

GUY. I have done.

HEN. You walk into a dance hall, on your own and dance?

SONNY. It's maybe not called a dance hall any more . . .
  missus . . . (*Invites her to say her name.*)

HEN. It's Henrietta.
  My name is Henrietta.

GUY. I've never met anybody called Hen / rietta.

HEN. / A a a. Hen'll do fine.
  (*To* GUY.) So what do you call a dance hall, then?

GUY. A club.

MISSY. And they let you into clubs on your own?

GUY. As long as you look okay and you've got ID.
  In fact, sometimes you've a better chance of getting in if
  you're on your own.

HEN. We used to go out in a crowd.

PETAL. And the first big trouble comes when he discovers
  they're going to get a place of their own and the doctor
  chappie isn't going to marry her. But Missy twists her dad
  round her finger and much as he's against the whole
  arrangement, he's comforted by the fact that they're only
  moving a couple of streets away and she isn't giving up her
  job or anything like that. But he's on the lookout now, for
  signs of trouble because he's not sure that Missy is in good
  hands.

GUY. There are still crowds, especially girls.

HEN. We had a mixed crowd

SONNY. so you always had someone to dance with.

MISSY. Do girls come in on their own?

GUY. They can do.

MISSY. But not many.

GUY. It depends where it is.
  But no.
  Not many.
  But they can.
  That's the difference.

HEN. You always could.
  It's just not a lot of fun.

JIM. What do you go for?

GUY. The dancing.

HEN. Show us.

GUY. I can't.
  I need music.

SONNY. It'll be that loud bumph bumph bumph stuff.
  Won't it?

GUY. Yeah.

HEN. I heard somebody say that that kind of music . . .

GUY. Dance?

HEN. . . . that it works because it catches our own internal
  beats.

GUY. I never heard that.
  It's too fast.

MISSY. Maybe you're thinking heartbeat.
  But what if other things inside you have other beats.

GUY. I can't hear them.

HEN. No but.

SONNY. I'm with you.

HEN. What if your heart's going boom boom boom

SONNY. but your
  Your

JIM. kidneys

SONNY. are going puh puh, puh puh, puh puh

HEN. And your
    Your

MISSY. spleen

JIM. is going mmcha mmcha, mmcha mmcha, mmcha mmcha.

> SONNY *and* HEN *and* JIM *work at this rhythm. The rain begins to sparkle.*

PETAL. But they genuinely love each other – my mum and dad – they certainly have loving moments and on one of those I see them, I catch sight of them before I'm born and I want to be part of that so next thing she knows, Missy is pregnant. Too soon for Doctor Kildare as my grandpa calls him now. Doctor Kildare thinks he doesn't want a baby and Missy doesn't know what to do, but she doesn't tell her Dad because that would be the end of everything.

GUY. There's something missing.

MISSY. Your liver.

HEN. What's your liver doing?

SONNY. It's too busy trying to cope with all the drugs and alcohol.

GUY. I don't take drugs.
    Climbing does it for me.

SONNY. You need focus up a mountain.

GUY. Yes you do.

MISSY. Show us your dance, then.

JIM. We'll be the music.

GUY. It's ridiculous.

JIM. // I did it.

MISSY. // I did it.

GUY (*to* HEN). I haven't seen anything from you.

HEN (*to* SONNY). I don't mind dancing.

SONNY. I'm a bit rusty.

HEN. And we'd need a tune.

MISSY. I don't know any of those old tunes.

JIM. I might be able to hum an old tune.

SONNY. Do you know any Glenn Miller?

JIM. Not that I could hum along to.
    I certainly don't know the words.

HEN. It wouldn't be appropriate anyway.

SONNY. // Sorry.

HEN. // Sorry.

JIM. What about a Burt Bacharach number?

HEN. Not my time.

SONNY. But if it had a beat we could do something.

HEN. Which Burt Bacharach number, then?

JIM. 'Blue on Blue'.

SONNY. Do you know it?

HEN. I'd need to hear it.

    JIM *sings 'Blue on Blue' and* SONNY *and* HEN *dance.*

PETAL. Right then my grandfather reaches down into the tin
    and lifts out the old Yale key. Missy gave him a spare key so
    that when she and Doctor Kildare were at work he could let
    in the meter readers and washing-machine engineers – they
    never had any luck with washing machines. One Sunday he
    pops over with some pudding that Hen made and nobody
    answers the door, but he can hear shouting and crying and
    he can see me on the floor. He's worried so he lets himself
    in, just as my father is making his way to the door and
    although my grandpa's first instinct is violent he notices a
    tear in my father's eyes . . .

SONNY. This is proper dancing.

GUY. I never said I didn't like it.

MISSY. He said he couldn't do it.

HEN. I could show you.

GUY. You've no idea how not tempted I am by that.

HEN. Is it that you're shy?

MISSY. Don't embarrass him.

SONNY. But we've all had a go.

JIM. That's true.

GUY. I'm on my way to climb a mountain. Did I not say? I
   only stopped to speak to you because you looked so wet and
   bedraggled, and I thought I recognised the girl who came
   with you . . .

   MISSY *turns to look towards the bathroom.* PETAL *listens.*
   PETAL *smiles.*

SONNY. Me too.

GUY. . . . and I should be going before I start to lose the light.

HEN (*trying to distract her attention away from* PETAL).
   Missy.

MISSY. . . .

   HEN *grips* MISSY*'s hand.* HEN *has never known anything
   before, not really, but right now she loves her daughter
   above everything and has begun to understand that right
   now is when they will lose* PETAL, *and* MISSY *needs help
   to get through it.*

HEN. Missy, we can't let him off that easily, can we?

MISSY. What?

HEN. We can't let him go till he shows us his dance.

MISSY. What?

HEN. His dance. It wouldn't be right if we didn't watch.

MISSY. No.
   Yes.

JIM. Absolutely.

HEN. Okay, here's the deal.
    You do one of your dances, or you learn a new one with me.

GUY. I couldn't.
    Seriously.

MISSY. He's shy.

SONNY. Or is it that you're too concerned about how you
    look?

GUY. It could be that.

HEN. He's young.

PETAL. . . . and in that instant my grandpa decides that even
    though he doesn't know my father as well as he'd like to, he
    is going to help him. Partly he's helping him because his
    daughter loves him and he wants her to be happy but part of
    it is because he thinks they might have a connection, given
    time and a bit of effort. So he stands in front of him and
    places his hand on his shoulder so that my dad has to look
    into his face. My grandpa looks straight at him and he says,
    'This is the hardest time. It gets easier. I'll help you.' Not
    knowing that no one has ever said that to my father, not his
    own father, or grandfather, no one. And he was running
    away because he couldn't do it all on his own. Right there
    in the hallway he crumples and as he goes down, he sees me
    and realises that, of course, the one thing he's always
    wanted, was his daughter, and he swears there and then that
    he'll never leave us.

GUY. I think I'm worried about how I'd look.

JIM. We could help you forget that.

HEN. How?

JIM. . . .

SONNY. What about if you imagine you're old?

HEN. I'm old.
    I mind how I look.
    I still do things.

SONNY. Yes but you're brave.

HEN. Thank you.

GUY. I'm not a coward.

SONNY. Not up high, you're not.

GUY. Or in the street.

MISSY. People are afraid of different things.

HEN. Do the dance once and we'll never mention it again.

GUY. I don't know what to do.
I don't know whether to dance on my own or with one of
you.

MISSY. I'm not much use.
I do a kind of vague seventies thing, shifting my weight
from one foot to the other in a bouncy sort of a way.

JIM. I could show you a short tap routine.

GUY. Tap's quite extreme, though, isn't it?

*He tries to get his body into a position where it might do
tap dancing.*

Way too extreme.

HEN. I'll dance with you.

GUY. But who'd lead?

HEN. I could have a go at leading.

SONNY. Have you done it before?
It takes a certain knack.
A bit of practice.

PETAL. My grandfather takes the key and the rusty nail and
puts them back in the tin. 'But what about the silver
threepenny?' I say. 'How did that change your life? You said
all three things changed you life.' And he smiles and says,
'Oh this is the best one of all, because it didn't just change
my life once, it changes it regularly. Why, all I have to do is
put it in my mouth and put this little girl on my knee and
watch her face light up in surprise every time it pops out.

Well, this little silver threepenny is worth a king's ransom.
Don't you think?'

PETAL *puts the tin back in her pocket.*

SONNY. I tell you what.

GUY. No, I know what you're going to say.
The answer is no.

SONNY. It'll only feel foolish at first.

GUY. I'm not dancing with you.

SONNY. We had to do it at school.

JIM. Yes we did.

SONNY. And you just got on with it.

HEN. Who led?

SONNY. Whoever was told to lead.

HEN. So you've been the leader and the led?

SONNY. I'm tall, I was mostly the leader . . .

JIM. Huh.

SONNY. . . . but not always, so I know what it feels like.

JIM. It only feels awkward till you learn the steps,

SONNY. after that it's just following.

GUY *and* SONNY *face each other to dance.* SONNY *puts*
GUY*'s arms in the right position.*

A bit of music here.

JIM (*sings*). Blue on blue.

GUY. Nope.
Nope.
Can't do it.

HEN. It's the music.

MISSY. He needs something a bit faster.

JIM. Like what?

MISSY. I don't know.
I'm hopeless with songs.

GUY. I can't do it.

HEN. Wait a minute.
Wait a minute.

HEN *starts singing 'I Wanna Be Loved by You'.* SONNY
tries to dance with GUY *but can't do it for laughing.*

GUY. Right.
That's it.

MISSY. She didn't mean to upset you.

JIM. It was just a joke.

SONNY. It was funny.

GUY. But I was being open.

MISSY. So he was.

GUY. I wasn't supposed to be ridiculed.

HEN. I'm sorry.

GUY. You should be.
A woman of your age.

HEN. I beg your pardon.

GUY. Got you.

PETAL. And any time I'm stuck or in trouble I can call on him
and say, 'Hey Grandpa, could you help me out this one last
time?' and he'll say, 'That's what you said the last time' and
just when I think he isn't coming and I'm all on my own
he'll turn up and give me his hand and say 'Come on, Fleur'
(my mother had been reading *The Forsyte Saga* just before
I was born but my Grandma Hen refused to call me anything
as highfalutin as Fleur, so she called me Petal). 'Come on,'
he says. 'This is the hard part. It gets easier after this.'

GUY. And now it's your turn.

MISSY. Who?

GUY. All of you.
    You want to see me dance?

MISSY. Go on, then.

GUY. Right, Sonny, you're the heart . . .

SONNY. Are you sure?

GUY. . . . and the heart goes

SONNY. boom, boom, boom.

GUY. Right.

JIM. I'm the kidneys, right . . .

GUY. Oh yes.

JIM. . . . . puh puh, puh puh, puh puh, puh puh.

MISSY. I'll be the spleen, then.

GUY. Oh no.
    Hen is the spleen.

HEN. Oh what?

GUY. Spleen.

    HEN *sighs.*

    Yes you are.

HEN. The spleen, then.

GUY. And the spleen goes . . .

HEN. I don't remember.

GUY. Tut tut.

HEN. I honestly don't remember, son.

GUY. Guy. My name is Guy . . .

SONNY. Some Guy, eh?
    Some guy, that Guy.

GUY. . . . which is why I never tell anyone. My mother read
    French stories and called me Guy. In French it's Gee, but

Guy was hard enough to live with. I didn't have the heart to change it.

JIM. No.

MISSY. I like it.

HEN. You would.

MISSY. Yes, I would.

GUY. And the spleen goes?

JIM. mmcha mmcha, mmcha mmcha, mmcha mmcha, mmcha mmcha.

GUY. Hen?

HEN. mmcha mmcha, mmcha mmcha, mmcha mmcha, mmcha mmcha.

GUY. Okay.
Ready?

MISSY. Wait a minute.
What about me?

GUY. You're the DJ.

SONNY. You have to conduct.

MISSY. Oh my god, I'll be terrible at this.

HEN. Just do it.

They try to put together all the sounds and when it starts to resemble music, GUY *dances.*

PETAL. 'Come on,' he'll say. 'This is the hard part.'

PETAL *reaches out her hand and walks through to the other side of the glass. She walks to where she can see them all having fun.*

'It gets easier after this.'

MISSY *sees* PETAL, *and then* HEN *sees* PETAL.

MISSY. // Oh there you are

HEN. // Oh there you are

PETAL. they say, not realising I've gone.
    Yes, I'm here.

MISSY. You were a while.

PETAL. 'It takes me a while,' I say.

JIM. // We were waiting.

SONNY. // We were waiting.

GUY. // We were waiting.

MISSY. // We were worried.

HEN. // We were worried.

PETAL. But it's all right.
    Look.
    I'm here now.

MISSY. // Yes.

HEN. // Yes.

JIM. // Yes.

SONNY. // Yes.

GUY. // Yes.

A picture of PETAL *becomes clear on the outside of the summer room.*

JIM. Did somebody mention tea?

End.

A Nick Hern Book

First published in Great Britain as a paperback original in 2004
by Nick Hern Books Limited, 14 Larden Road, London W3 7ST
in association with the Traverse Theatre, Edinburgh

Shimmer copyright © 2004 Linda McLean

Linda McLean has asserted her right to be identified
as the author of this work

Cover image: Euan Myles, featuring Lesley Hart as Petal

Typeset by Country Setting, Kingsdown, Kent CT14 8ES
Printed and bound in Great Britain by Bookmarque,
 Croydon, Surrey

A CIP catalogue record for this book is available from
the British Library

ISBN 1 85459 702 7